Depression Solutions

Therapy, Natural Treatments, or Medication?

Maria Lloyd

Copyright 2010 by Mental Health Press

ISBN 0-974-31061-1

ALL RIGHTS RESERVED. No part of this book may be reproduced, stored in a retrieval system, or transmitted by any other means: electronic, mechanical, photocopying, recording, or otherwise, without prior written permission of the copyright holders.

Printed in the United States of America

Cover design by Laura Fortin

Author photograph by Mindy Webb

Copyediting by Manju Vatsh

Book layout by Laura Fortin

DISCLAIMER/LEGAL NOTICES: This book is supplied for information purposes only and, as experienced in this subject matter as the contributor is, the material herein does not constitute professional advice. The information presented herein represents the view of the contributors as of the date of publication.

Because of the rate with which conditions change, the contributor reserves the right to alter and update their opinion based on the new conditions. This book is designed to provide accurate and authoritative information with regard to the subject matter covered. It is sold with the understanding that the publisher and the contributors are not engaged in rendering medical, pharmaceutical, legal, or other professional advice.

If medical or pharmaceutical advice or other professional assistance is required, the services of a competent professional should be sought. The reader is advised to consult with an appropriately qualified professional.

The contributor, Maria Lloyd, MFT, does not accept any responsibility for any liabilities resulting from the personal decisions made by purchasers of this book. Any perceived slights of specific people or organizations are unintentional.

For additional information on Maria Lloyd, please visit www.marialloyd.com or email at maria@marialloyd.com.

Maria Lloyd LMFT #38399

Acknowledgements

I'm filled with gratitude for the love and support of family and friends. Thank you for believing in me and encouraging me to write this book. My husband Dave, your outpouring of love, grace, and true friendship are an amazing blessing to me. My two boys, Gabriel and Jacob, you are my precious gifts from above and bring me an abundance of joy and reminders to live in the moment.

I'm thankful to the many people that have supported my writing. Mom and dad, your hours of proofreading drafts, provision of valuable feedback, and constant encouragement gave me the strength and support I needed. Christina, your friendship is a rare treasure. Thank you for listening, laughing with me, and helping me stay connected and grounded. Linda, your consistent wisdom and gentle ways of challenging me promote much needed growth. Susan, your professional feedback and support as a therapist has been of great value to me. Gina, you advocated for me and kept me calm along the way. Carol, your insight and helpful suggestions moved me forward. Catherine, you helped me believe in this project at the right time. Heidi & Karen, your weekly prayers for many years laid the foundation for this book.

Thank you to my professors and colleagues at U.C. Davis and Fuller Seminary's School of Psychology. You gave me knowledge and experience, laying the groundwork for my work with clients and writing.

I acknowledge Jerome A. Motto for his contribution to this book as a friend and psychiatrist. Your professional knowledge and life experience helped me formulate my thoughts around the diagnosis and treatment of depression, especially regarding hard to treat cases.

Thank you to each of my clients. You entrust me with your innermost thoughts and feelings and provide an opportunity for me to learn from each of you.

Finally, nothing would be possible without my faith and relationship with God. You are the ultimate healer and source of hope. Thank you for giving me the vision and desire to create this book.

Table of Contents

Preface: The Journey Out of Depression

1. **Life is not Black and White, Neither is Treatment** 1
   Why is There a Higher Incidence of Mental Health
   Disorders Today? 2
   The Consequences of Not Getting the Right Treatment 3
   Is This Book Biased? 5
   What's the Secret to Effective Treatment? 6

2. **The Facts about Depression** 8
   Major Depressive Disorder 13
   Dysthymic Disorder 20
   What Causes Depression? 27

3. **What to do First: Setting Treatment Goals** 39
   Determine if you have Depression 39
   Find a Therapist Who's Right For You 41
   How To Screen Your Therapist 44

4. **What to do Next: Working with your Therapist** 48
   What to Expect From Your Therapist 49
   What are the Most Effective Forms of Therapy Used Today? 50
   How Much Therapy Do You Need? 58
   Which Treatment is Right For You? 60

5. **Medication vs. Natural Treatments: Behind the Controversy** 61
   What are Psychotropic Medications? 61
   What are Natural Treatments and Complementary and
   Alternative Medicines? 62
   What's All the Controversy About? 64

6. **Which Treatments are Most Effective for Depressive Disorders?** 69
   Psychotherapy 70
   Natural Treatments 73
   Pharmaceutical Treatments 80

Table of Contents

7. **Developing Your Treatment Plan** 95
   Working With Your Therapist 95
   How We Discover What Works 96
   Guidelines for Developing the Treatment Plan 97

8. **Resilience: The Ultimate Stress Solution** 105
   How to Boost Your Stress Management Skills 109
   How Resilient Are You? 113
   Strategies for Boosting Your Resilience Factor 114

9. **Improving Yourself** 118
   Take Steps Toward a Healthier You 118

10. **Science and the Effect of Genes on Depression** 134
    What are Genes and What Do They Do? 135
    How Risky Is "Genetic Risk?" 144
    Can Your Personal Genome Predict Genes for "The Blues"? 144
    Charting Your Own Mental Health History 145

11. **How to Help Someone who Needs Treatment** 148
    The Breakdown: Managing a Crisis 151
    If You Believe Someone is Suicidal 152

12. **Conclusion: The Truth Shall Make You Free** 158

Appendix: 161
   Depression Quiz: Self-Questionnaire 161
   Medical and Mental Health History 164
   Emotional/Relational History 165
   Mood Chart 166
   Treatment Goal Planning Worksheets 168

Bilbliography 170

Preface:
The Journey Out of Depression

The clinical world is full of treatments for depression. And chances are, for every treatment you discover, your research will reveal hundreds of opinions proclaiming its miraculous effectiveness...and hundreds of opinions discrediting it.

But here's the truth: None of these opinions can tell you whether or not that treatment will work for you.

Perhaps you've been grappling with these questions: Am I Depressed? Do I need therapy? Do I need medication... or will natural treatments work for me?

Unfortunately, there is no one treatment that's guaranteed to work for everyone — for any psychological disorder. After all, life is complicated, and so is treatment.

With so much misinformation out there, choosing the right path out of the wilderness can be daunting, confusing, and even frightening. It's no wonder that many people remain untreated, for years in pain and misery. Others suffer chronic depression for decades, skipping from one treatment to the next and never getting better when their symptoms were treatable: if only they knew what that right treatment was.

Choosing the wrong treatment can have negative consequences, such as exacerbating the illness, or creating a new illness altogether. As a therapist, I've seen people waste thousands of dollars and several years of their lives on failed treatments, enduring the heartache of never getting better, thinking: Others get better... why don't I?

That's why I wrote this book. I've counseled hundreds of people desperate to find relief from their depression. I found out that people who are given the right support and information make better decisions and have more effective treatment outcomes for depression. Seeing people change and feel better has been a catalyst for me to learn all I can to help them.

My own struggle with depression also nurtured my passion to equip others with the help they need. Ten years ago, my physical and emotional health was deeply affected by the stress of two difficult pregnancies and starting a private practice. Even though I was a trained therapist, I thought my low mood was due to stress and didn't seek help until my symptoms got worse. Finding the right treatment was not as simple as I thought it would be. I spent a lot of time and energy in a trial and error process that eventually resulted in a combination of treatments. Thankfully, with the right help, my hope was gradually restored, as well as my functioning and ability to experience joy. I know what it's like to feel hopeless and wonder if the pain will ever go away. And I want to encourage you to believe that your happiness and contentment can be improved.

The good news remains--there is hope. The fact that so many treatments for depression exist mean that people are being helped and the likelihood of you finding symptom relief is high if you are willing to do the work required.

This book will help you learn how to:
- Determine whether you need therapy, and learn how to choose the right therapist
- "Screen" a therapist, and know whose opinion to trust
- Decide whether you may be a candidate for natural treatments, or whether you're likely to need medication now
- Weigh the realities of treatment side effects of both pharmaceutical and homeopathic therapies
- Set realistic treatment goals and properly monitor your progress to determine if a particular therapy needs to be adjusted, complemented by an additional therapy, or replaced altogether
- Develop a balanced treatment approach that will dramatically improve your short and long-term prognosis

Perhaps you're reading this book because you want someone to simply tell you what to do. This book will not do that. What this book will do is give you the strength and assurance to trust your instincts and empower you to make healthy choices that have a lasting impact on your mental health. If this book is too difficult to read by yourself because of the debilitating effects of depression, enlist a loved one to read it with you and support you in this process.

For each reader, Depression Solutions: Therapy, Natural Treatments or Medication? will be both a journey of self-discovery and a roadmap to a healthier, happier future. I encourage you to begin this venture with an open mind. During the time you are reading this book, forget what you've read before, let go of what others have told you in the past. Try to set aside your preconceived notions about what works and what doesn't.

What do you need to do to feel better? Let's find out.

1
Life is Not Black and White, Neither is Treatment

Most people like simple problems with easy solutions. It would be nice to have someone tell us what to do rather than tolerate uncertainty and have to wrestle through the muck of decision-making as we try to answer the questions, "Should I go this way or that way?" or, "Who is right and who is wrong?"

Does there have to be a "right" or a "wrong"? It's true that no two people experience life in the same way. It's the same with mental illness. For example, the Diagnostic and Statistical Manual or DSM, which mental health professionals use to diagnose people, lists criteria which define the different diagnoses. However, even though I have treated many people diagnosed with Major Depression, I have never seen anyone who has the exact same symptoms as the other. This is the great lesson of psychotherapy: Different people truly do experience life in a different way and manifest different symptoms.

Research has shown us that psychological disorders result from a combination of genes, neurochemistry, environment, personality, and other developmental factors. We come from different gene pools and different environments. We have different physiologies and chemistries. We've each experienced different stressors throughout our lives, and we've developed varying levels of emotional resilience to cope with those stressors.

So, it's no surprise that treatment doesn't come in "one-size-fits-all." Finding the right treatment means finding the treatment that's right for you.

If you suspect that you or someone you care about is suffering from a depression, you're not alone. Depression is no respecter of age, ethnicity or socioeconomic class. Mental health disorders are so common that, in any given year, one in four American adults suffer from a mental health disorder that could be diagnosed and treated.

One thing is certain, though: more of us are taking psychotropic medications (the umbrella term that includes antidepressants) than we were a decade ago. Since 1996, this number has increased 73 percent among adults. What's fueling the dramatic rise in drug treatments? The most commonly cited causes are expanded insurance coverage and primary care doctors' increasing familiarity with medication for depression and other mental health disorders.

The incidence and prevalence of diagnosed mental health disorders has in fact increased over the past few decades; certainly this is true for depressive disorders. But, are more of us suffering from depression than ever before?

Why is There a Higher Incidence of Mental Health Disorders Today?

Stress, the Great Instigator: The stress of daily living has increased, and with it, as you might guess, the incidence of depression. Stress, in one way or another, contributes to all mental and physical health problems. We have learned that even mild depression can have a dramatic impact on our health and well-being.

Most surveys suggest that the amount of stress experienced in coping with our more complicated, modern lives has nearly doubled over the past three decades. We are simply living more stressful lives and this is taking an enormous toll on our health. We're certainly living busier, more competitive lives. We are required to be ambidextrous jugglers. Every day we find ourselves juggling work, family, and community obligations, and not always as competently as we'd like it to be. At least a third of us have trouble keeping all the balls in the air on a daily basis. And for a person who's trying to cope with depression, this juggling act can become extremely overwhelming.

Stress negatively impacts us in many ways: it increases anxiety and depression, raises tension in our close relationships, increases health problems, and fuels mental health problems. Increased stress loads can drive us toward unhealthy stress management behaviors that further fuel already existing health problems; for example, smoking, using alcohol or drugs, junk food and comfort eating. Handling stress in unhealthy ways might alleviate symptoms of stress in the short term, but, over time, we end up creating more emotional and physical health problems and, ironically, more stress.

The Consequences of Not Getting the Right Treatment

Depression can be disabling, and when its victims receive either no treatment or the wrong treatment, their lives can quickly spiral out of control. Often, the story doesn't end well for people not fortunate enough to get the treatment they need. Some people languish for years in misery and despair. Countless others endure an impoverished quality of life, never knowing true peace and contentment, never achieving their full potential. And we can never lose sight of the high mortality rate associated with mental illness, much of which can be attributed to suicide.

Suicide is a preventable health problem. Yet, every year, around 33,000 people in the U.S. die by suicide; in fact, suicide is the eleventh leading cause of death in the general population. Every 42 seconds someone attempts suicide. Every 17 minutes an attempt is successful. For every completed suicide, there are 8 to 25 attempted suicides. I'm not sharing these statistics to cause alarm. But more to educate that more than 90 percent of those who committed suicide had a diagnosable psychological disorder, most commonly — and perhaps most disturbingly — a depressive disorder or substance-abuse disorder. These disorders are treatable; and those deaths were preventable.

How does it ever go so far? If you trace the arc of these tragedies, you'd find one common thread: The treatment wasn't working, or there was no treatment at all.

Symptoms, when left untreated, tend to escalate. Over time, they last longer and become more severe. A person who might currently be subclinical for depression (i.e., doesn't meet the full diagnostic criteria for the disorder) is at risk for developing a full-blown clinical disorder. And with any disorder, as symptoms progress and worsen, it becomes more difficult to treat, which means that recovery will take even longer.

Further complicating matters, roughly half of those with one mental disorder also meet the criteria for two or more disorders.

Severity of symptoms is strongly related to co-morbidity (co-occurrence of multiple disorders). In other words, the co-morbidity itself increases the severity of all symptoms. For example, substance abuse exacerbates depression; depression exacerbates anxiety; anxiety exacerbates AD/HD.

Depression steals minds, souls and lives — sometimes overtly, and sometimes like a thief in the night…slowly, day by day, week by week. And the ripple effect can be devastating. Mental health problems lay waste to relationships and careers, wreaking havoc with what makes us most human: our emotions, our relationships, our ability to trust our judgments about those closest to us.

We humans are highly adaptable; evolutionarily, we've had to adapt to survive. We tend to adapt to our symptoms and come to believe that this is simply how life must be, or at least, this is how our lives will be. We forget what it felt like to feel good. We fall victim to our own cognitive distortions — we lose the ability to objectively evaluate ourselves, a symptom which often manifests as low self-esteem, feelings of worthlessness, and guilt. We slip into a persistent negative feedback loop; constantly circling our personal misfortunes, misinterpreting neutral or trivial daily events as yet more evidence of our personal defects, perhaps even assuming responsibility for negative situations that are completely beyond our control.

In a troubled mind, thoughts, beliefs and fears get blown out of proportion so easily that it becomes harder to recognize that those distortions are just a byproduct of disorder. The person begins to believe that no one loves them; after all, how could anyone love someone so worthless? And often, "the problem" is never discussed, never acknowledged, never treated.

Unfortunately, the stigma that has sometimes been attached to depression hasn't made it any easier. Some people who suspect that they need help don't seek it for fear that acknowledgment will cost them their jobs or relationships, that they'll be perceived as "weak" or hopelessly flawed. It's no wonder that so many people who suffer mental health problems have avoided seeking treatment, bravely continuing to deny, avoid, marginalize or rationalize their symptoms — both to others and to themselves.

Life is not Black and White, Neither is Treatment

In the past, stigma not only deprived people of the treatment they desperately needed, but also deprived them of dignity, and of the joy of fully participating in society. But the good news is that stigmatization is gradually dissolving. Today, nearly 70 percent of Americans say they wouldn't be concerned if someone found out they were seeking help from a mental health professional.

The modern mind-body view of psychological disorders as a combination of physical and psychological dysfunction has helped dissolve the stigma. And destigmatization, fortunately, has increased the number of people who want to seek treatment.

Is This Book Biased?

Perhaps you're reading this book because you don't want to take medication. You're not alone. No one does. But here's the reality: Some people require medication to get better — it's that simple. But some don't. For others, natural treatments, such as herbal remedies or dietary supplements, are enough. Still others achieve the best results through combination therapies that may include, for example, therapy, medication, natural treatments, and adjunct treatments such as yoga or acupuncture.

Medication vs. natural treatments. The public debate rages on, pitting these two treatment modalities against each other as bitter rivals, as if they were candidates from different political parties, as if the choice is black or white — you can only choose one.

The Internet, alone, has been both a boon and a danger to objective psychoeducation. While there are websites that provide useful guidance, many are either biased, oversimplified, or inaccurate. They may exist solely to induce visitors to buy a product or service that's "guaranteed" to relieve your symptoms of depression.

How do you know whose advice to trust? In order to get the right answers, you must ask the right questions. For each of the medications and natural remedies covered in this book, we'll cover the current known contraindications and side effects to help you analyze your own risk factors and to guide you when consulting with a doctor.

You'll find that this book, at every turn, offers a balanced approach to evaluating treatment options. You'll learn how to weigh the pros and cons of each treatment. And you'll be better equipped to follow your instincts when making choices since you will have the knowledge you need to make a good decision.

You will only find one biased recommendation in this book, and that recommendation is this: Start with a therapist. If you need therapy to get better, neither medication nor natural treatments will address the psychological root causes of your problems. If you have a thorn in your side, you can take painkillers to inhibit the pain, but unless you remove the thorn, you will never be free of painful symptoms. You will never be free.

Practically everyone who suffers from depression needs some level of support from an objective mental health professional. If nothing else, everyone can benefit from — and, in some cases, require — a therapist's oversight during treatment. A competent, experienced therapist can help you uncover and resolve underlying psychological issues that might be causing or contributing to symptoms, as well as help you develop a safe and balanced approach to treatment.

Around twenty percent of people who take medications for depression will not require therapy or any other treatment. The other eighty percent will need some level of support from a professional therapist to get better and stay healthy. Emotional health, for all of us, is a journey, not a destination. Therapy can help you learn new coping mechanisms and strategies and help you build long-lasting emotional resilience that could help smooth out the bumps along the road.

What's the Secret to Effective Treatment?

The first thing you should know, as you begin this process, is that the effectiveness of any treatment — pharmaceutical, natural, or therapy — always depends on these factors:
1. An accurate psychological assessment or diagnosis
2. An accurate assessment of your complete health picture, including any coexisting medical conditions or other underlying physiological causes of psychological problems

3. Your specific neurochemistry, neurobiology and genetic predispositions
4. Your willingness to adhere to an effective treatment plan and to actively participate in the process of getting better

The tools and exercises in this book will help you assess your symptoms, analyze your options, and determine what your next step should be.

In the world of mental health treatments, there's no room for black-and-white thinking. There are few treatment certainties that apply to every one of us… except these three:

One: If you don't manage your depression, it will manage you.

Two: Treatment offers hope for recovery from even the most severe forms of depression.

Three: Hope is our greatest asset.

2
The Facts About Depression

What is depression? The short answer is that depression is a "mood disturbance," typically experienced as significantly lower than normal mood for an extended period of time. The complete answer gets a little more complicated.

In assessing whether you or a loved one is suffering from depression, it's important to distinguish between normal and abnormal mood fluctuations. Everyone experiences some degree of depression throughout their lives — and, for that matter, euphoria, as well. We all have our "up" days and "down" days. But these mood swings are not necessarily indicative of a psychiatric condition that requires treatment.

For most of us, these extreme feelings are transient, and typically pass within a day or two. It's when these feelings linger for weeks, months or even sometimes years, consuming your thoughts day in and day out, that the condition becomes clinically significant. For the person suffering from depression, these mood swings become so invasive that they interfere with daily life.

In a nutshell: The diagnosis of a Mood Disorder, such as Major Depression, is dependent on the intensity and duration of the mood disturbance, its accompanying symptoms, and the degree to which it interferes with a person's functioning in both social and occupational settings.

Depression infiltrates every nook and cranny of your life, coloring your view of the world. And that color, too often, is gray. Receiving that big promotion you've worked so hard for may not feel much different from getting a good parking place at the mall. Conversely, losing that promotion may not feel much worse than burning your toast at breakfast.

One of the least discussed aspects of severe clinical depression is that the deepest, darkest depression is not experienced as melancholy or sadness. The most severe — and most dangerous kind of depression is numbness, a complete absence of feeling and a loss of concern for yourself and for others. Depressed people ultimately stop expecting positive outcomes. And even when something good happens, they're often unable to recognize it, and too numb to enjoy or appreciate it.

If you or someone you love is struggling with depression, you may feel that you're alone. You're not. Clinical depression plagues every population across the globe, and it takes a monumental toll in human suffering. Depression is so common that it has been referred to as the "common cold of mental illness." But far more devastating than the common cold, depression impairs a person's ability to function well which could last a lifetime, if left untreated.

To get a true picture of depression's grasp on the population, consider these statistics…

- Roughly 20% of the population will experience some degree of depression during their lifetime.
- An estimated 5.8% of men and 9.5% of women worldwide will experience a depressive episode in any given year (World Health Organization).
- At any given time, nearly one in ten people is experiencing symptoms of major depression in the U.S. population (Compton & Kotwicki, 2007).
- 10 to 25 percent of women and 5 percent to 12 percent of men will become clinically depressed and experience a Major Depressive Episode, or develop Major Depression at some point in their lives (DSM-IV-TR).

Depression is currently estimated to cause the largest amount of non-fatal health burden worldwide, accounting for 12 percent of all total years lived with disability (Hassad 2006). In other words, more people are living with depression than any other non-fatal illness. We can live with depression, but we do not live with it unharmed.

Who is at Risk for Depression?

The short answer? Everyone. All of us. Each of us. No one is immune. Depression can happen to a person of any gender, age, race, or socioeconomic level.

But in general, people who have experienced any of the following are at a higher risk for depression:
- A previous depressive episode.
- A family history of depression
- Difficult childhood, especially a history of physical, sexual or emotional abuse
- Substance abuse problem
- Single, with no significant other.
- Recent bereavement
- Women who have recently given birth
- Recent serious medical conditions, such as stroke, heart attacks, diabetes.
- Recent trauma, such as assault, military service or witnessing a fatal accident
- Recent severe stressors, such as divorce or loss of employment
- Women are at significantly greater risk than men for developing Major Depressive Episodes at some point in their lives. Depressive episodes occur twice as frequently in woman as in men.
- In general, depression is more common among those who are less resilient, and those who have not developed good coping skills.

What are the symptoms of depression?

No two people experience depression exactly the same way. In Noonday Demon, author Andrew Solomon encapsulated the varying faces of depression like this: "Like snowflakes, depressions are always unique, each based on the same essential principles but each boasting an irreproducibly complex shape."

The clinical community classifies depression as a mental health disorder, but depression takes a physical toll as well. Many depressives, for example, suffer back problems, headaches, and weakened immune systems. Some depressed people can actually feel a change in their bodies. Some may experience a churning feeling, particularly people who are anxious or agitated depressives. Others experience a sensation of "heaviness", feel lethargic and even physical pain. Some have difficulty digesting food.

Recurrent depression can be such a vicious cycle that the line between cause and effect blurs... Is the psychological symptom causing the physical symptom, or is the physical symptom causing the psychological symptom? Depression typically presents with both psychological (mind and emotions) and somatic (biological and physiological) symptoms.

Ultimately, there is no such thing as a "mind-body split." Our mental states and physical states are inextricably bound. The psychological or cognitive symptoms of depression — what we think about — are just as important as the physiological ones, and any diagnosis and treatment plan must address both.

Psychological (mental/emotional) symptoms of depression may include:
- persistently low mood
- low self-esteem and low self-confidence
- pessimism and negative outlook
- a sense of despair
- hopelessness and helplessness; feelings of worthlessness
- thoughts of suicide
- irrational feelings of guilt

Depressives also typically suffer from anhedonia, or loss of pleasure in activities they used to enjoy. Somatic (biological and physiological) symptoms, may include:
- fatigue and lack of energy
- an inability to concentrate or make decisions
- sleep difficulties; either too much or too little sleep
- sexual dysfunction, such as loss of sex drive
- change in appetite, weight gain or loss
- psychomotor activity changes, such as slower movements or speeded up, agitated movements

Loss of pleasure is nearly universal among depressed individuals. More than three-fourths report trouble with sleep. Often, depressives awaken early in the morning, long before it's time to arise. Others may actually eat and sleep more than usual. Many will have lost their appetite and weight. In many cases, mood is significantly worse in the morning, then improves somewhat as the day wears on, a condition known as diurnal variation.

Depressed people usually complain of fatigue, which they may report as tiredness or loss of energy. Speech and movements may be slower than normal. You may notice a marked pause before they answer questions or initiate action that has been requested. This is called psychomotor retardation. Speech may be very subdued, even inaudible. Some depressives even stop speaking completely, except when responding to a direct question.

Many depressives drink more when they become depressed.

Depressives lose the ability to objectively evaluate themselves, a symptom which often manifests as low self-esteem, feelings of worthlessness, or guilt. Guilt may include unrealistic negative evaluations of one's worth, or guilty preoccupations with and ruminations over minor past failings. They may slip into a persistent negative feedback loop, constantly circling their personal misfortunes. They may misinterpret neutral or trivial day-to-day events as evidence of personal defects. They may assume an exaggerated or even inappropriate sense of responsibility for negative events. For example, a sales representative may blame herself for failing to sell a product that has no market. The sense of worthlessness or guilt may even be of delusional proportions.

Many depressed individuals become cognitively impaired... unable to think, organize, remember information, or make decisions. They may be easily distracted, and unable to concentrate on the task at hand. People who are suffering from severe clinical depression also may exhibit symptoms of thought disorder, which includes disorganized thinking, indecisiveness, impaired memory and judgment, and a tendency to completely misinterpret events negatively.

What are the different forms of depression?

The most common forms of depressive disorders are Major Depressive Disorder and Dysthymic Disorder. Some forms of depressive disorder include slightly different characteristics, or they may develop under unique circumstances. Such forms of depression might include: Postpartum Depression, or Seasonal Affective Disorder (SAD).

Clinical depression occurs in episodes, which may last from days to months, or in the most severe cases — years. Major Depressive Episodes, chained together over time, become the building blocks of a full-blown Depressive Disorder. Major Depressive Disorder is diagnosed when someone experiences one or more Major Depressive Episodes.

In some individuals, Major Depressive Episodes can occur as part of a cycle of mood changes that cycle from extreme highs (mania) to extreme lows (depression), known as Bipolar Disorder (also called manic-depression). In addition to depression, Bipolar Disorders can include Manic, Mixed, or Hypomanic Episodes, a milder form of mania.

About 5 to 10 percent of individuals with Major Depressive Disorder subsequently develop a Manic Episode. It's important to note that people with a bipolar disorder can be misdiagnosed as Major Depressive, particularly if they have prominent depression and mild mania or hypomania. If you notice mood shifts from slightly elevated to depressed, contact a physician or psychiatrist for complete assessment. For someone who has bipolar disorder and is misdiagnosed as having depression, being placed on the wrong medication can create a mood cycling problem that is much harder to treat. The importance of an accurate diagnosis cannot be over-emphasized.

Major Depressive Disorder

"The most awful thing about depression is that it's hard to recognize it when you're in it. I just knew that I was unable to talk in a normal way to friends and family about anything, let alone about how awful I felt. Many of my waking hours were filled with morbid thoughts. It was like having a big black, invisible cloud following me everywhere I went."

Major Depressive Disorder, also called major depression, is

characterized by a combination of symptoms that interfere with a person's ability to work, sleep, study, eat, and enjoy once-pleasurable activities. Major Depression is disabling, and prevents a person from functioning normally.

A Major Depressive Episode is characterized by at least two weeks of depressed mood and/or loss of interest in normal activities, accompanied by at least four other symptoms of depression. A Major Depressive Episode is the core syndrome of clinical depression. It is not a codable psychological disorder in itself; rather, it is one of the building blocks of a Mood Disorder (e.g., Major Depressive Disorder or Bipolar Disorder). Major Depression may occur only once in a person's lifetime or in recurrent episodes, broken by periods of remission. Major Depression does tend to have a devastatingly high rate of recurrence. Consider these statistics:

- At least 60% of people who experience a single Major Depressive Episode can be expected to experience a second episode
- People who have had two episodes have a 70% chance of experiencing a third episode
- People who have had three episodes have a 90% chance of experiencing a fourth episode

You can see why early diagnosis and treatment is crucial. Left untreated, depression can spiral into a vicious cycle of debilitating episodes that recur again and again throughout a person's lifetime.

Symptoms of a Major Depressive Episode usually develop over days to weeks. A Major Depressive Episode may be preceded by what's known as a prodromal or preliminary period that includes anxiety and mild depression symptoms. This prodromal period can last for weeks or even months before the onset of a full-blown Major Depressive Episode.

The median age of onset is 32. An untreated Major Depressive Episode typically lasts for 4 months or longer, regardless of age or onset. In 70 to 80 percent of cases, there is a complete remission of symptoms and functioning returns to normal. In 20 to 30 percent of cases, some depressive symptoms remain, though they are insufficient to meet the criteria for a Major Depressive Episode. These symptoms may persist for months or years.

In general, the more symptoms a person has, the more likely it is that a diagnosis of Major Depressive Episode is warranted. Following are the criteria used by therapists to diagnose a Major Depressive Episode...

Criteria for Major Depressive Episode

To warrant a diagnosis of Major Depressive Episode, the episode must be severe enough to cause significant distress or impairment in a person's work performance or social life. The impact on a person's occupational functioning may be the hardest to detect because earning a living is so important that most people will go to great lengths to hide symptoms that could threaten their employment.

A. In the same two-week period, the person would have had *five or more* of the following symptoms, which represent a definite change from the usual functioning. **Either depressed mood or decreased interest or pleasure must be one of the five.*

- **Mood.** For most of nearly every day, the person reports depressed mood (e.g., feels sad or empty) or appears depressed to others. (e.g., tearful). Note: In children and adolescents, depression can present as irritable mood.
- **Interests.** For most of nearly every day, interest or pleasure is markedly decreased in nearly all activities (as noted by the person or by others), including activities that the person normally enjoys doing. The person may lose interest in work, hobbies, and sexual activity.
- **Eating & Weight.** Although the person is not dieting, there is a marked loss or gain in weight (e.g., 5% in one month) or appetite, markedly decreased or increased nearly every day.
- **Sleep.** (Nearly every day, the person sleeps either excessively or doesn't get enough sleep. (Insomnia or hypersomnia) Even if sleeping excessively, the person often still feels tired.
- **Observable Psychomotor Activity.** Nearly every day, others can see that the person's activity is sped up or slowed down.
- **Fatigue.** Nearly every day, there is tiredness or loss of energy.
- **Self-worth.** Nearly every day, the person feels worthless or

inappropriately guilty. These feelings are not just about being sick; they may be unwarranted.
- **Concentration.** As noted by the person or by others, nearly every day, the person is indecisive, or has trouble thinking or concentrating.
- **Thoughts about dying.** The person has had repeated thoughts about death (other than the fear of dying), or about suicide (with or without a plan), or has made a suicide attempt.

B. **Substance Exclusion.** Regardless of the severity or duration of the symptoms, Major Depressive Episode should not be diagnosed if the disorder is directly caused by a general medical condition, or by the use of substances, including prescription medications.

C. **Bereavement Exclusion.** Major Depressive Episode should not be diagnosed if the episode began within two months of the loss of a loved one. There is, however, an exclusion for the bereavement exclusion: If the symptoms are unusually severe, a Major Depressive Episode may be diagnosed, regardless of the time elapsed since the death of a friend or relative. Examples of severity might include: severely impaired functioning, severe preoccupation with worthlessness, ideas of suicide, delusions or hallucinations, or slowed psychomotor activity.

Any person who has experienced a Major Depressive Episode(s) may, at a given point in time, also be in full or partial remission. Partial Remission means that the person now has either fewer than five criteria symptoms, or has had no symptoms for less than two months. Full Remission means that the person has exhibited no evidence of Major Depressive Episode during the past two months.

Postpartum Depression (PPD)

Giving birth is one of the most remarkable and life-changing events a woman will ever experience. However, women can be particularly vulnerable to depression after giving birth as well as during pregnancy, when hormonal and physical changes — added to the new responsibility of caring for a newborn — can be overwhelming. It takes a little time for them, as well as their husbands, to adapt to the new member of the family.

Following the birth of the baby, up to 80 percent of new mothers experience a brief episode of the "baby blues." Baby blues is a transient condition that occurs within 3 - 10 days following childbirth. For women who have a strong emotional support system, the baby blues vanish within 1 to 2 days.

But 12 to 16 percent of new mothers will develop Postpartum Depression (PPD), also called Post-Natal Depression (PND), a much more serious depressive condition for which active treatment and emotional support are required. More and more, we're finding that PPD often serves as the trigger for lifelong major depression.

Some women are at greater risk for Postpartum Depression than others. For example, women who have:
- Experienced prior Mood Disorder, such as Major Depressive Episodes or Mania
- Experienced anxiety and depression symptoms during pregnancy, or the baby blues following childbirth
- A family history of a Mood Disorder, such as depression, anxiety or bipolar disorder.

Postpartum Depression is diagnosed when a new mother has a Major Depressive Episode within one month to one year following the birth of the baby, and can develop gradually or suddenly. Postpartum Depression symptoms may include:
- Total loss of enjoyment in life (anhedonia)
- Feelings of helplessness and despair
- Abnormal maternal attitudes, which can vary widely from disinterest and fear of being alone with the baby, to obsessiveness with the baby's well-being and even over-intrusiveness that doesn't allow the baby to properly rest.

Consider the story of Brook Shields, whose 2005 book Down Came the Rain detailed her battle with Postpartum Depression.

"At first I thought what I was feeling was just exhaustion, but with it came an overriding sense of panic that I had never felt before. Rowan kept crying and I suddenly began to fear the moment when Chris would bring her back to me. I started to experience a sick sensation in my stomach; it was as if a vice was tightening around my chest. Instead of the nervous anxiety that accompanies panic, a feeling of quiet devastation overcame me. I hardly moved. Sitting on my bed, I let out a deep, slow gutteral wail. I wasn't simply emotional or weepy like I had been told I might be. This was something different. This was sadness of a shockingly different magnitude. It felt as if it would never go away."

Antenatal Depression (Depression During Pregnancy)

"Why wasn't I looking forward to meeting my baby? I thought these were supposed to be the happiest days of my life. When I thought about the future, I only felt gloomy. Then I felt guilty for feeling apathetic."

While less talked about than post-partum depression, a startling 10 to 20 percent of women struggle with symptoms of depression during pregnancy, and one-fourth to one-half of them will experience symptoms consistent with Major Depression. Pregnancy is supposed to be one of the happiest periods of a woman's life, but many women find themselves trapped in cycles of confusion, fear, sadness, stress, and depression.

Factors that increase the risk of antenatal depression include:
- Family or personal history of depression
- Relationship problems
- Previous pregnancy loss
- Infertility treatments
- Stressful life events
- Pregnancy complications
- History of abuse or trauma

Unfortunately, antenatal depression is not always properly diagnosed because it can masquerade as "just another hormonal imbalance." It's important to seek early diagnosis and treatment because depression impacts the health of both the mother and the baby. A woman who is depressed may not have the strength or desire to adequately care for herself or her developing baby. Untreated depression can lead to poor nutrition, drinking, smoking, or other self-destructive behavior, which can cause premature birth, low birth weight, and developmental problems.

Psychotic Depression

"I kept feeling that I was going to be punished. Somebody was after me. I've done so many bad things in my life. Now it was time to pay..."

In some severe cases of Major Depression, a person may exhibit psychotic symptoms. Psychotic Depression occurs when the depressed person loses contact with reality; that is, hearing, smelling or feeling things that others can't detect (hallucinations); and having strong beliefs that are false, such as believing you are the president or that the devil is speaking to you (delusions).

These psychotic features can be either mood-congruent (for example, a depressed man feels so guilty that he imagines he has committed some heinous sin) or mood-incongruent (for example, a depressed woman believes she is being persecuted by the FBI). If you suspect that you have psychotic depression, seek help from a mental health professional immediately.

Seasonal Affective Disorder (SAD)

"Every year, I dread winter because I know the sadness will set in. My light box helps a little, but most of my energy, motivation and excitement for life disappears with the sunlight."

In its usual pattern, Seasonal Affective Disorder (SAD) is characterized by the onset of depression during the winter months, when there is less natural sunlight. For most people, the depression generally lifts during spring and summer. Winter depressives may report symptoms such as physical pain or craving for carbohydrates.

The diagnostic criteria for SAD include:

- Major Depressive Episodes should have regularly begun during a particular season of the year
- Complete recovery should also have occurred regularly during a particular season
- These seasonal changes should have occurred in each of the previous two years, with no other nonseasonal depressive episodes

SAD may be effectively treated with light therapy, though roughly half of those with SAD don't respond to light therapy alone. Antidepressant medication and psychotherapy can reduce SAD symptoms, either alone or in combination with light therapy.

Dysthymic Disorder

"For eight years I was unable to escape this low-level depression, which I now know is dysthymia. You don't notice it at first... it's so gradual. What I do know is that I slowly but surely transformed from being a person who had a joy and passion for life to a person who was most often sad and pessimistic. Gradually, sneakily, that sadness becomes the norm. Since I was still able to work, I didn't think it was something I could change or get help for. I can't believe how much better my life is, thanks to medication and therapy."

Dysthymic Disorder, also called Dysthymia, is chronic, long-term depression, characterized by at least two years of depressed mood for more days than not. People with Dysthymia exhibit many of the symptoms found in Major Depressive Episodes. However, the symptoms of Dysthymia are less severe and may not disable a person, though they can prevent a person from functioning normally. Dysthymia is also distinguished from Major Depression in that it does not include thoughts of death or suicidal ideation.

Dysthymic Disorder occurs in approximately 6% of adults

over the course of their lifetime. The median age of onset is 31. Because dysthymics suffer quietly and are not severely disabled, the depression is often not noticed or diagnosed unless it escalates into a Major Depressive Episode. In fact, after the dysthymic person receives treatment, it often seems to observers that the person has undergone a "complete personality change."

Criteria for Dysthymic Disorder:

A. On the majority of days for two years or more, the person reports depressed mood or appear depressed to others for most of the day.

B. When depressed, the patient manifests two or more of these symptoms:
   • Decreased or increased appetite
   • Decreased or increased sleep
   • Fatigue or low energy
   • Poor self-image
   • Reduced concentration or indecisiveness
   • Feelings of hopelessness

C. During this two-year period, the above symptoms are never absent longer than two consecutive months.

D. During the first two years of this syndrome, the patient has not had a Major Depressive Episode, Manic, Hypomanic or Mixed Episode, Cyclothymic Disorder.

E. The symptoms are not directly caused by a general medical condition or the use of substances, including prescription medications.

F. The symptoms must cause clinically important distress or impair work, social or personal functioning.

How gender, culture and age impacts depression

Are the distinctive qualities of each individual's depression determined by biological differences between men and women?... between the very young and the very old?... between Asians and Europeans?...between gay and straight people? Or are they determined more by what we call sociological differences, in other words, differences due to the expectations that society impose on people according to the population they happen to live in or represent?

The answer in every case, is both. Depression is always contextual, and must be interpreted within the context in which it occurs.

Gender

Men and women often experience depression differently, and each gender has different coping mechanisms. In general, men tend to externalize symptoms; whereas, women tend to internalize symptoms. Let's take a deeper look...

Men

While men in our culture are learning to be more emotionally expressive, they still tend to mask their pain, and resort to self-defeating ways of managing their emotions. They're victims of Be Strong syndrome: Big boys don't cry. Men are more likely than women to engage in destructive, often addictive, behaviors when they're depressed, such as turning to alcohol or drugs, or becoming frustrated, discouraged, irritable, angry and even abusive. Many have trouble managing anger so they bite back on it until they can't take it anymore and explode. They may even neglect and abuse spouses and children.

Many walk around with a vast hurt inside and a longing for someone to heal it. But they're also ashamed of those feelings, so they don't let anyone know. Always expecting rejection, they would attempt to make the rejection first, as a defense mechanism.

Some men become "workaholics" to avoid thinking about their depression and avoid discussing how they feel with family or friends.

Others engage in reckless, risky behavior, such as engaging in illicit love affairs. Overt depression may only emerge when addictive behaviors no longer assuage the emotional pain, or once a man's defenses have been unmasked.

Rather than confronting their real feelings, men are more likely to acknowledge having fatigue, irritability, loss of interest in once-pleasurable activities, and sleep disturbances. And even though more women attempt suicide, a greater percentage of men actually commit suicide. In fact, almost four times as many males than females die by suicide. While women often commit suicide as a result of a relationship breakdown, men typically commit suicide because they lack goals, feel a lack of purpose in their lives, or cannot "fix" a problem.

Women

Case Vignette:

"It wasn't until Jamie was about five months old that I started feeling sad. I had just separated from Jamie's dad and I'd gone back to work. Jamie went to day care, but it was overwhelming, trying to care for an infant, run the household and juggle the demands of my career.

Jamie was still waking up two or three times every night, and it seemed that he caught one illness or another from day care every couple of weeks. The combination of physical and emotional exhaustion sent me into a tailspin.

I wouldn't let anyone help me with the baby because I couldn't admit defeat, couldn't admit that I was struggling just to get through the day. I didn't tell anyone I was crying myself to sleep, when I was lucky enough to get some sleep. People kept telling me I was supposed to enjoy these precious moments with my son. But I no longer felt any sense of joy. And I felt horribly guilty about that.

The biggest step for me — the hardest step — was admitting to other people (and to myself) that I needed help."

Women, more than men are likely to admit to feelings of sadness, worthlessness and excessive guilt — all hallmarks of depression. Women are also willing to discuss their feelings with family and friends. While this support is often helpful, women are more prone than men to becoming trapped in a cycle of despair, helplessness and passivity.

Women also often report feeling less appreciated by their partners than men do. In addition to workplace stress, a woman may bear a greater burden for housework and childcare than do men. Some women must also cope with the additional stress of caring for aging parents, abuse, poverty, and relationship problems.

Chronic stress provokes chronic rumination — the churning of feelings over and over again. Rumination can help perpetuate stress because it depletes the reservoir of motivation, perseverance, and problem-solving skills that is required to facilitate positive change. Chronic rumination provokes more chronic stress… you can see the vicious cycle.

Women between the ages of 18 and 45 comprise the majority of those with major depression. In the United States, Major Depressive Disorder is twice as common in adolescent and adult females as in adolescent and adult males. This increased differential in women emerges during adolescence, often coinciding with the onset of puberty.

While, biology alone does not account for the high rate of women's depression, biological, life cycle, hormonal and psychosocial factors unique to women are linked to women's higher depression rate. Researchers have shown that hormones directly affect the brain chemistry that controls emotions and mood. For example, many women report worsening of depression symptoms several days before the onset of menses. Some women are susceptible to a severe form of premenstrual syndrome (PMS), sometimes called Premenstrual Dysphoric Disorder (PMDD). PMDD results from hormonal changes that typically occur around ovulation, and before menstruation begins. In fact, many scientists believe that the cyclical rise and fall of estrogen and other hormones may affect the brain chemistry that is associated with depression. Some women experience an increased risk for depression during the transition into menopause.

Age
Older adults
Many have come to believe that depression is "a normal part of aging." It's not. In fact, studies suggest that most seniors feel satisfied with their lives, despite the fact that, as they age, they experience more physical ailments.

However, older adults are more likely to be suffering from more serious medical conditions such as heart disease, stroke or cancer — all of which commonly cause depressive symptoms. Older adults may also be taking more medications which can have side effects that contribute to depression. Because of these health reasons, depression affects 1 in 5 older people living in the community, and 2 in 5 living in nursing homes.

Some older adults experience ischemia, a condition in which the blood vessels become less flexible and harden over time, constricting the flow of blood to the body's organs, including the brain. The result is what's often referred to as vascular depression. In addition to increasing the risk of serious cardiovascular illnesses, constricted blood flow contributes to depressed mood and thought disorder. The brain abnormalities resulting from vascular depression can also prevent depressed older patients from responding to antidepressant medication.

Children and adolescents
Childhood depression often persists, recurs, and continues into adulthood, especially if the depression has gone untreated. This history of childhood depression tends to be a predictor of more severe disorders in adulthood.

Before puberty, boys and girls are equally likely to develop Depressive Disorders. By age 15, however, girls are twice as likely as boys to have experienced a Major Depressive Episode (NIMH, 1999).

A depressed child or adolescent may pretend to be sick, refuse to go to school or work, cling to a parent, or worry excessively that a parent may die. Older kids may sulk, get into trouble at school or work, be negative and irritable, and feel "misunderstood." While these symptoms can simply be normal mood swings typical of adolescent developmental stages, consistent patterns of such behaviors bear constant watching.

Adolescent depression can also lead to an increased risk for suicide. Suicidal ideation or thoughts of suicide is alarmingly high among adolescents. Some research indicates that one in four 15- to 24-year-olds report to have entertained suicidal thoughts to general practitioners. Even more alarming, most of these adolescents did not appear to have noticeable depressive symptoms (Hassad, 2006).

Depression in adolescence comes at an already tumultuous time of personal change. Both boys and girls are forming an identity distinct from their parents, grappling with gender issues and emerging sexuality, and making decisions for the first time in their lives.

Adolescent depression frequently occurs simultaneously with other disorders such as anxiety, disruptive behavior, eating disorders or substance abuse.

Race/Ethnicity

It's important not to dismiss or misinterpret a potential depressive symptom merely because it's not the norm for one's own culture. Culture can influence both the symptoms of depression and the way those symptoms are experienced and communicated.

For example, in some cultures, depression may be experienced largely in somatic or physical terms, rather than in terms of feelings, such as sadness or guilt. Latino and Mediterranean cultures often express depression in terms of physical complaints, such as "nerves" and headaches. Chinese and Asian cultures complain of weakness, tiredness or "imbalance." Middle Eastern cultures complain of problems of the "heart." Some Hopi Indians may express the depressive experience as being "heartbroken."

What Causes Depression?

There is no single cause of depression. Like the symptoms of depression, its etiology or causes vary from person to person. In fact, depression can be caused by a combination of factors, including biological factors, personality and environmental factors, and psychological maturity factors, such as whether or not the person has developed effective coping skills.

Let's take a look at some common causes of depression…

Neurological and chemical causes of depression

Brain Chemicals: Neurotransmitters

Changes in brain chemistry influence mood and thought processes. Depression is believed to result from changes in brain chemicals, specifically the neurotransmitters. Neurotransmitters act as chemical messengers that send messages from one nerve cell to another, facilitating communication between the brain and the rest of the body.

During depression, quantities of the neurotransmitter serotonin, in particular, are significantly reduced. Serotonin promotes social confidence and a feeling of well-being. If serotonin levels are high, your confidence soars, and you feel less vulnerable. If serotonin levels are low, you may feel helpless, become defensive and less willing to take risks.

Serotonin also plays a key role in helping us maintain a proper perspective of events; for example, serotonin modulates rejection sensitivity. Lower serotonin levels can cause depressed people to be acutely sensitive to rejection.

Gamma-aminobutyric acid (GABA) is another neurotransmitter thought to play a role in causing depression. GABA, working in tandem with serotonin, acts as an inhibitory neurotransmitter that quiets the stress response when a person thinks about stressful events.

Stress Hormone: Cortisol

Cortisol is a stress hormone that can provoke depressed mood. In people who are depressed, cortisol is produced in excess, and it's responsible for much of the physiological damage caused by long-term stress.

Often, depressives aren't aware of what triggered their depression. How does this happen? When a memory or live event triggers depression, feeling is separated from thought. The depressive loses the thought, but the feeling keeps on churning. This is why you'll often hear depressives say "it just came out of the blue," when, in fact, depression rarely "comes out of the blue."

Here's how this psychological discontinuity happens neurologically...

The conscious, second-by-second processing of verbal conversation happens in one part of the brain (the prefrontal lobes of the neocortex), while your emotional evaluations are happening in another part of the brain — in the limbic system, which is a network of brain structures involved in learning, memory, motivation and generating emotions.

When you hear a stress-inducing sentence, two things happen: (1) Your language and working memory centers decode the meaning and insert the meaning into the conscious mind; (2) A subcortical system triggers a stress response — your limbic system launches a cascade of events that sends chemicals — including cortisol — racing throughout your body. Terrorist attacks and recessions, for example, would spike cortisol surges.

Prefrontal lobe activity — conscious, intelligent processing of the sentence —happens in nanoseconds. But the emotional system lags behind for seconds, even minutes. So, there's still cortisol floating in the bloodstream thirty seconds after the news vanishes from working memory, yet you no longer remember what triggered the depressed mood. For example, you may be listening to the radio and hear a song that was playing in the background five years ago at the very moment that you were told that a loved one had been killed in a car accident. You unconsciously associate the memory of your past traumatic experience with the song, triggering a depressed mood.

Brain structures that play a role in depression

The amygdala and the hippocampus are a pair of small brain structures that work in tandem to generate emotions, attach emotions to memories, and store and index those memories.

The almond-shaped amygdala is the brain's emotion factory, the "gut feeling" center. The amygdala is an evolutionary brain structure that's always on the alert, looking for danger. It registers events and directs your evaluation of the event, then provokes you to respond. In other words, the amygdala tells you how you should feel about something, how it relates to your history, and how you should respond. The amygdala sends signals that are integrated with maps that are stored in memory by the hippocampus.

Located beside the amygdala is the hippocampus, a small brain structure shaped like a seahorse. The hippocampus is the brain's spatial memory bank. You can think of it as a memory map room that stores and keeps track of memories, much like the directory system on a computer hard drive.

The map room is a specialized part of our memory bank whose contents are stored right next door to emotion central — the amygdala. Some scientists believe that the amygdala is able to somehow mark memories created by other parts of the brain as being "emotionally significant." That's why our sense of place is tied to our recollections of our experiences and our sense of comfort or unease in the world.

Severe stress impedes our ability to form memories. fMRI (Functional Magnetic Resonance Imaging) studies have shown that the hippocampi of depressives are smaller than those of individuals with no history of depression. Why does this matter? A smaller hippocampus supports fewer feel-good serotonin receptors. A serotonin deficit, remember, can trigger depression.

Some researchers believe that depressed individuals may simply be born with a smaller hippocampus, which would predispose them to suffer from depression. And some believe that extended release of the stress hormone cortisol is toxic to the hippocampus' ability to form memories. (WebMD, 2006)

Extended release of the other stress hormones, such as glucortocoid, actually cause hippocampus nerve cells to atrophy. During a traumatic event, for example, a person's stress response weakens the hippocampus so much that the memory never forms, even though the amygdala — emotion central — still managed to capture the essence of the traumatic event. But the result is an incomplete emotional memory — a "flashbulb memory" — which may help explain why the specific traumatic memory has a tendency to disappear from consciousness, while persisting in our gut reactions, phobias, and of course, ultimately depression.

The good news is that nerve cell atrophy in the hippocampus is reversible, if the stress ends.

Psychosocial Stressors

Psychosocial stressors are stress-triggering events that impact various aspects of our social and psychological behavior. Clinical depression can be triggered by a severe psychosocial stressor.

The most common psychosocial stressors in adult life include the breakup of intimate romantic relationships, death of a family member or friend, economic hardships, racism and discrimination, poor physical health, and assaults on physical safety. But other more subtle factors that impact a person's sense of identity or self-esteem may contribute to depression; for example, a job demotion, or a spouse who constantly belittles and criticizes.

Psychosocial stressors play a more significant role in triggering the first and second Major Depressive Episodes, but less of a role in triggering subsequent episodes.

Bereavement and Loss

Few losses in life can compare to the death of a loved one. The death of a child or spouse during early or mid-adult life is far less common than divorce, but generally is a far more powerful depression trigger. And unfortunately, people are generally unlikely to seek professional treatment during bereavement, unless the severity of the emotional and behavioral disturbance is incapacitating.

Common symptoms associated with bereavement include crying spells, appetite changes and weight loss, sleep disturbances, poor concentration, and ruminations on sad thoughts and feelings. Bereaved people may also suffer unwarranted guilt, believing they could have prevented the death.

Stress and traumatic events

Although some stressors are so powerful that they can trigger depression in most otherwise mentally healthy people, the majority of stressful life events don't necessarily trigger mental disorders. Rather, such stressful events are more likely to trigger mental disorders in those who are vulnerable biologically, socially, and/or psychologically.

Individuals who are at greater statistical risk for depression as a result of stress and trauma include women, young and unmarried people, African Americans, and individuals with lower socioeconomic status (NIMH, 1999).

A life-threatening accident or physical assault (e.g., mugging, robbery, rape) frequently provokes emotional and behavioral reactions that jeopardize mental health. In the most fully developed form, this syndrome is called Posttraumatic Stress Disorder, or PTSD. Women are twice as likely as men to develop PTSD and possibly depression following life-threatening traumas.

Normal, but significant life transitions can also trigger depression; for example, moving, school graduation, changing jobs, losing a job, getting married or divorced, retirement.

Troubled Relationships

Depression wreaks havoc with what makes us most human…our relationships, our attitudes, our ability to trust our judgments about those closest to us. Repeated plunges into depression lay waste to marriages, friendships and careers.

Depression insinuates itself into our relationships, causing a ripple effect that touches every corner of our lives. Depression is both caused by — and a cause of — poor relationships. One of the bitter ironies of depression is that depressed people crave connection to other humans, but the nature of the disorder makes it difficult to connect. Depressives often can't state their needs directly, keeping secret wishes locked in their hearts.

Relationship problems place a chronic strain on a person's day-to-day emotional well-being. Relationship problems might include unsatisfactory intimate relationships, conflicted relationships with parents, siblings, and children, and "falling-out" with work colleagues, neighbors and friends.

Sometimes depressed people don't realize they're depressed, and are oblivious to the impact of depression on themselves, as well as the people around them. Unfortunately, depressives are often not much fun to be around. And to add insult to injury, they usually feel very guilty about that. They often feel (and are actually) ostracized by others, which, to a depressed person, may seem to be yet more evidence of his or her personal defects, further fueling a cycle of guilt, shame and sense of hopelessness and worthlessness... fueling a vicious, recurrent cycle of depression.

It's no wonder that many depressives deny, avoid, marginalize or rationalize their symptoms. They're almost invariably concerned about confidentiality, fearful that acknowledgment of these symptoms will cost them relationships, jobs, or respect. And, in a particularly cruel twist of irony, a general lack of motivation — a common symptom of depression — contributes to preventing someone from asking for help.

Depressives are missing a part of the self that contains a positive self-image. They have no reliable reservoir of self-esteem. As a result, they're overly dependent on love, respect, and approval from the significant people in their lives. In fact, they're often dependent on constant positive feedback about themselves, whereas, someone who's not depressed needs only periodic maintenance of self-esteem, and isn't thrown for a loop by loss or reversal. When depressives don't get the positive feedback they crave, depression increases.

Sometimes it's tricky to pinpoint where the 'depression' is at work and where the psychological issues are at play. For example, is someone relying too much on his/her spouse for love and affection because he/she is codependent, or because he/she is depressed? Since there is often such a close interplay of the depression and psychological issues, it's extremely helpful to have a therapist involved in the treatment plan.

Sometimes this endless need is not obvious, and what's visible is a dependency on the symbols of love, respect and approval; for example, financial success, control or power. In fact, depressives often chase the symbols of success to fill the void inside. They may believe: "If I'm not a success, the people who are most important to me won't love me anymore."

Family Ties... Is there a genetic link to depression?

Scientists are beginning to identify genes that appear to contribute to depression. Major Depressive Disorder is 1.5 to 3 times more common among first-degree biological relatives. Children, siblings and parents of people with severe depression are much more likely to suffer from depression than are members of the general population. The interaction between genetic predispositions, stressful life events and our individual experiences play a role in causing depression, especially in women. Studies of depression suggest that genes play a greater role in contributing to depression in women than in men. The research suggests that genetic predispositions may be more likely to impact women's sensitivity to stressful life events, making them more susceptible to depression.

Family members do share common neurochemistry, but environment plays a huge role in causing depression, too. First-degree relatives live in the same household, share common beliefs and values, and are subject to the same stressors. When one family member suffers from severe clinical depression, other family members suffer; for example, they may withdraw and become socially isolated, which can contribute to depression later in adulthood. Children of depressives may also be more sensitive to rejection.

Negative thought patterns and outlook on life

Depression tends to cause people to withdraw socially. Isolation can help perpetuate the tendency to only see the negative aspects of one's life, to fall into negative patterns of thinking, and to ultimately come to expect only negative outcomes. Emotional well-being is associated with a positive — yet realistic — outlook on life.

Negative thought patterns often stem from prior negative experiences; and they can be reactivated by stressful, adverse life events. Prolonged negative thinking can become an endless feedback loop, one negative thought feeds another and another and another. Soon the person is ensnared in a downward spiral that leads to full-blown clinical depression.

Negative thinking usually leads to feelings of worthlessness and loss of self-esteem. Self-esteem is the abiding set of beliefs we have about our own worth, competence, and ability to relate to others. Self-esteem buffers us from adverse life events. Depressed people usually don't have that inner resource of self-esteem to help them through trying times.

Feelings of joy or pride can even evoke painful memories of past disappointments. A depressed person remembers the mother who was never satisfied, the father who didn't seem interested. The bereaved child within, who has never completed grieving for those incomplete relationships, continues to mourn up to this day.

Psychotherapists generally agree that the impact of a particular stressor is moderated by the personal meaning of the event or situation. Cognitive theories of depression emphasize that how we perceive and interpret stressful events helps determine whether or not those events will trigger depression. For example, a romantic breakup will trigger a much stronger emotional response if the affected person thinks: I am empty and incomplete without her love. Or: I will never find another who makes me feel the way he does.

Can you see how such thought patterns are distorted interpretations? The tendency to become depressed can be related to the tendency to attribute these three qualities to adverse events:

1. **Global Impact.** *This event will have a big effect on me.*
2. **Internality.** *This is my fault. I should have done something to prevent this.*
3. **Irreversibility.** *I'll never be able to recover from this.*

Negative thinking tends to instill feelings of helplessness, which worsens the depression. One prominent theory of depression holds that depression emerges when a person feels helpless and entrapped, a theory that stems from studies of learned helplessness in animals. In learned helplessness experiments, animals were trained in an enclosure in which shocks were unavoidable and inescapable, even if the animals attempted to escape.

When these animals were later placed in enclosures from which they could have easily escaped, the animals remained immobile and unable to learn avoidance maneuvers. Their previous learned helplessness made them indeed feel helpless and they came to believe that any attempt to escape would be futile.

· Depression and immune dysfunction

Severe, chronic stress depresses immune function. And immune dysfunction diminishes the body's capacity to fight diseases and disorders.

Chronic or long-term activation of the body's stress response leads to what is called allostatic load, which is a prolonged wear-and-tear on the body. Allostatic load levels are high in depressed and anxious people. Allostatic load's impact on the human body is similar to what happens to a car or appliance after years of wear-and-tear.

Allostatic load is associated with impaired immunity, accelerated atherosclerosis and increased incidence of type 2 diabetes, obesity, hypertension (high blood pressure), hyperlipidemia (excess of fats in the blood). Allostatic load is also associated with osteoporosis (bone demineralization), due to its chronically high levels of havoc-wreaking cortisol and atrophy of nerve cells in the brain.

This stress load includes inflammatory chemicals like cytokines, which have a significant impact on behavior and emotion. Cytokines are a regulatory protein that is released by the cells of the immune system and acts as a mediator between cells when the body is generating an immune response.

Cytokines can both produce symptoms of depression, and depress the immune system. Depression occur more frequently in those with immune disorders. Activation of the immune system induces sickness behavior such as apathy, lethargy, lack of motivation and appetite dysregulation — all of which are, you'll note, also symptoms of depression. Some cytokines activate adrenaline-like brain substances and serotonergic systems (involving serotonin) in ways that are similar to depressive symptoms.

Depression associated with general medical conditions

Up to 20 to 25 percent of individuals with general medical conditions such as diabetes, cancer, myocardial infarction or other cardiac conditions, carcinomas and stroke will develop Major

Depressive Disorder during the course of their general medical condition (DSM-IV-TR). And Major Depressives have been shown to have a high prevalence (65 to 71 percent) of the most common chronic medical conditions (NIMH, 1999).

Depression can also emerge in people who suffer serious injuries, particularly when the injuries result in chronic pain, such as back pain. Depression intensifies pain and physical suffering. It causes fatigue and a decrease in energy that tends to worsen over time.

And when a person is clinically depressed, managing the medical condition becomes more complicated, and the long-term outlook is less favorable. By the same token, a serious medical condition adversely affects the prognosis of a person who has Major Depressive Disorder. For example, a person who's juggling a serious medical condition is more likely to suffer longer depressive episodes, and not respond as well to treatment — particularly when the medical condition is chronic. People suffering from a chronic illness often have difficulty adjusting to the demands of the illness, while focusing on treatment.

Chronic illness often affects a person's mobility and independence, which can affect a person's self-identity — the way a person views himself or herself and relates to others.

Seeking a different — or what they perceive to be "less stigmatized" — explanation for their difficulties, some depressed people undergo extensive (and expensive) diagnostic procedures and are treated for other complaints, while the depressive disorder goes undiagnosed and untreated. On the other hand, certain medications and some medical conditions such as viruses or a thyroid disorder can cause the same symptoms as depression.

You can see how depression complicates diagnoses. While clinical depression may not cause the medical condition, it almost invariably makes them worse.

Common complications include:
- Problems with serious illnesses; e.g., heart disease, diabetes and cancer
- Exacerbated hypertension and arthritis
- Migraine headaches

- Severe backaches, abdominal or other pains
- Sexual dysfunction
- Sleep disorders
- Severe fatigue and loss of energy

Depression co-occurs with other psychological disorders

Depression may be caused by, or co-occur with (known as comorbidity) other psychological disorders. The following disorders often co-occur with clinical depression…

Anxiety Disorders. Depression often accompanies anxiety disorders, including: Panic Disorder, Obsessive-Compulsive Disorders, Phobias and Posttraumatic Stress Disorder.

Bipolar Disorders. Depressive Episodes, cycled with Manic Episodes is characteristic of Bipolar Disorders. There is a broad spectrum of symptoms for someone with bipolar. They may cycle from mildly depressed to mildly elevated.

Personality Disorders. Depressed mood is almost invariably an intrinsic element of Borderline Personality Disorder, and can accompany other personality disorders, such as Avoidant, Dependent, and Histrionic Personality Disorders.

Substance-Induced Mood Disorders. Nearly 30 percent of individuals who have substance abuse problems also suffer from Major Depression. Alcohol or other substances can cause depressed mood, as well as the elevated mood associated with Manic Episodes. Without treatment, substance abuse worsens the mood disorder. Alcohol abuse or dependence literally doubles the risk of major depression in people of all ages. Some research suggests that alcohol may even trigger a genetic marker for depression.

Cognitive Disorders. Depression is often comorbid with cognitive disorders such as Dementia and Alzheimer's Disease. Delirium can often begin with depression or anxiety.

Adjustment Disorders. Depression often coexists with adjustment difficulties as a way of adapting to life's stress. These individuals are generally tearful, sad, hopeless.

The causes of depression are not always immediately apparent. Depressive symptoms often become tangled with symptoms of other psychological or physiological disorders, so diagnosing a depressive disorder requires careful evaluation by a trained therapist or psychiatrist.

3
What to do First: Setting Treatment Goals

Self-education is empowering. The next few chapters will help you prepare for your journey of self-discovery, and ensure that you aren't forced to solely rely on physicians or therapists for information.

To obtain the best learning experience and the most accurate self-assessment, follow these steps in chronological order:

Determine if you have Depression

1. **Find Out.** If you believe you have symptoms of depression:
   A. First, take the Depression Self-Questionnaire in the Appendix to assess symptoms of depression you have concerns about. If you're having trouble objectively evaluating your symptoms, ask a friend or family member to help you answer the questions.
   B. If your results suggest that you may have symptoms of depression, begin charting your moods using the Mood Chart in the Appendix.

Set Treatment Goals

No matter which treatment you choose, this book will help you learn how to set realistic treatment goals and properly monitor your progress in order to determine whether a therapy needs to be adjusted, complemented by an additional therapy or replaced altogether.

What should you expect from any therapy? In setting goals, the first step is to distinguish between short-term and long-term goals. That's the key to establishing realistic and achievable goals. We live in a nanosecond society that can encourage unrealistic expectations in practically every aspect of our life. We've gotten spoiled. We expect everything to happen immediately.

Unfortunately, immediate cure only happens in the movies; real treatment solutions take time to work their magic. Look at it this way… it took longer than 24 hours to create the psychological problem you're dealing with, so doesn't it make sense that it will take even longer than 24 hours to fix it?

With treatments for depression, patience is a virtue. Many factors can cause a particular treatment to fail, but one of the most common reasons people with treatable disorders don't get better is that they fail to adhere to the treatment regimen. When recovery isn't happening as fast as we want it to, it's easy to be tempted to jump from one treatment to another, one extreme to another. For example, some people who need medication resist the idea of taking it for too long. Meanwhile, the symptoms become more and more severe. Then they finally agree to take medication, expecting an overnight cure that won't happen. Others bounce from medication to alternative therapies too quickly, without giving either enough time to work.

Setting realistic expectations for both the short-term and the long-term will help you choose therapies that are right for you, and give you the patience and fortitude to adhere to them.

Your hopes and dreams for living a fulfilled life may include goals that are intensely personal; if so, be sure to include those in your lists, too. No goal is too big or small. The objective of this journey of self-discovery is to emerge with a complete self-portrait. If you're having a hard time painting a complete portrait, don't fret. Your therapist can help you explore all avenues of your life and extend your horizons.

Where do you want to be in the short term…in the long term? Use the Worksheet in the Appendix to map out your Treatment Goals.

Your immediate goals should include:
1. Restoring stability and functionality (e.g., eliminating thoughts of suicide, enhancing occupational functioning, improving relationships)

2. Relieving the symptoms that are causing you distress; (e.g., sleeping difficulties, prolonged sadness)

3. Making choices that put you on the path to accomplishing your long-term goals

What to do First: Setting Treatment Goals

Your long-term goals might include:
1. Making the pain go away. This one can take time. Recovering from loss, working through old pain and rebuilding relationships requires reflection and "processing" time.
2. Improve self-esteem, sense of self-worth and increase feelings of confidence
3. Improve problem-solving and decision-making skills
4. Improve coping skills and feeling more in control
5. Resolve any sense of loss (e.g., loss of a job, career, money, family)
6. Restructure thought patterns and eliminate negative self-talk or faulty internal chatter and dialogue
7. Develop a better support system such as family, friends, community groups, support groups
8. Implement a healthy living regime — improve eating patterns, nutrition and sleep hygiene
9. Enhance self-actualization — the drive that directs your growth and development — to achieve your highest potential and live a fulfilled life

These goals are just examples to get you started. Your own list may be entirely different. It may be simpler, or more complex — no list is too short or too long. Your therapist will work with you to establish realistic goals.

Find a Therapist Who's Right For You

Psychotherapy, or therapy, involves talking to a trained mental health professional (such as a psychiatrist, psychologist or counselor) to discover what's causing your symptoms and implement effective strategies for managing them.

Choosing a therapist is a bit like choosing a romantic partner. While you and your therapist (hopefully) will not be mating for life, you WILL become partners. Recovery is a partnership.

Successful therapy is collaborative and always focused on empowering you to make good choices — now, and for the rest of your life. The therapist will guide the therapy process, and support you as you make important changes in your life — both large and small. But the interesting thing about therapy is that success ultimately depends on you.

In other words, the therapist helps you learn how to help yourself.

To get the maximum benefit from therapy, you must stay motivated to work hard. The most effective therapies are those that revolve around client choice and participation. A good therapist will motivate you to actively participate in — and take responsibility for — 'getting better.' The more you can do to help yourself, the greater your odds of long-term success.

The first secret to choosing the right therapist is this: Choose a therapist you feel comfortable talking with. If you don't feel comfortable with the first therapist you talk to, choose another one.

Great therapists understand the indispensable value of client-therapist rapport, and they'll refer you to another therapist if the relationship is not a good fit. Professional honesty is an important quality to look for in a therapist. Trust is essential. A therapist should also be willing to refer a client to other professionals if they're not trained to handle any aspect of the client's treatment.

All therapists are not created equal. Scanning the websites of different therapists will reveal a confusing alphabet soup of acronyms--MD, PhD, LMFT, MSW, PsyD, to name a few. Credentials are important; they're evidence that the therapist has received a certain level of training. But credentials aren't everything. Sometimes people with top-notch credentials make dreadful therapists. One of the most important qualities of a good therapist is the ability to listen and care, which can't be achieved through formal education and training.

Now let's take a look at the distinctions between different kinds of therapists:

Psychiatrists. (MD degree) Psychiatrists have medical and pharmaceutical training and are licensed to prescribe drugs; psychiatrists should, in fact, be experts on issues regarding psychotropic medications. They specialize in testing (particularly neuropsychiatrists), diagnosing, and treating mental or psychiatric illnesses. They're also trained in psychotherapy, though many only provide treatment for medication and refer clients to another clinician for therapy.

Psychologists. (Doctoral degree — PhD or PsyD) Psychologists are experts in the study of the human mind and human behavior. They're also trained in counseling, psychotherapy, and psychological testing (particularly neuropsychologists), and they're good at helping you uncover emotional problems that you may not realize you have. Psychologists primarily use cognitive-behavioral therapy in treating clients, which helps people identify and change distorted and damaging thought patterns in order to change behavior. (See CBT discussion in Chapter 3) Psychologists are not licensed to prescribe drugs, so they often work closely with a client's primary care physician or a psychiatrist.

Licensed Professional Counselors, Marriage and Family Therapists. (LMFT, LPC) Counselors have attained at least a master's degree in counseling and 3,000 hours of supervised experience. They're licensed to diagnose and treat a wide range of mental health problems, including depression, anxiety, substance addiction and abuse, suicidal impulses, stress-related problems, self-esteem issues, and interpersonal relationship problems, such as parenting and marital discord. They often work closely with other mental health specialists, such as a psychiatrist who can prescribe medication.

Social Workers. (LCSW) Social workers specialize in providing social services in health-related settings, which are often governed by managed care organizations. They provide counseling for interpersonal relationship problems and work to improve and maintain a person's psychological and social functioning. Social workers specialize in helping people improve functioning in their particular social contexts or environments.

Child and Adolescent Therapists. In the mental health profession, there are fewer child and adolescent therapists than therapists who are trained to work with adults. But it's often important for children and adolescents to see a therapist who specializes in treating their age group; or at least, has several years of experience working with kids.

How To Screen Your Therapist
I'm ready to talk to a therapist... Where do I start?
Collect names:
- Ask trusted friends and colleagues for recommendations.
- Visit the American Psychological Association and American Psychiatric Association websites to obtain lists of therapists.
- If your insurance policy will only cover certain therapists, obtain your managed care or insurance provider's entire list of covered therapists — not just a handful of names. Ask friends and colleagues if they know a therapist who can recommend a therapist from the provider's list.
- Call the Psychiatry or Psychology Department of a reputable University and ask for recommendations on therapists who were trained in their program.
- Call large psychiatric clinics and try to speak to someone who's knowledgeable about each therapist's areas of specialty and can recommend a therapist who may be a good match for you.

Do your research
- Visit the websites of therapists whose names you collect.
- Go shopping. Therapist "shopping" is perfectly acceptable.
- Talk to potential candidates on the phone to pre-screen and get a feel for whether you're likely to have rapport with this therapist.

You may need to talk to several therapists before you find The One. But if you or someone you're intervening for is in crisis (e.g., having thoughts of harming yourself or someone else), call the National Suicide Hotline at 1-800-273-TALK, call 911, or go to the nearest emergency room.

Before you make an appointment with a therapist, do some basic screening to rule out therapists with whom you are unlikely to have good rapport and/or who may not have the right qualifications to treat you. Often, you can get answers to important 'dealbreaker' questions in the initial phone consultation.

Possible questions to ask:
- What is your definition of therapy or counseling?
- What are your credentials and qualifications?

What to do First: Setting Treatment Goals

- How long have you been in practice?
- How extensive is your experience working with issues similar to mine?
- What are the benefits of therapy?
- How many sessions would you anticipate for a client like me?
- Please describe your general approach to therapy. What is your modality/orientation and how does that impact me?
- What would you consider to be a realistic outcome for me? What are the odds of short-term, and ultimately long-term success? What constitutes 'success' or 'effective treatment' to you?
- How do you view our respective roles during therapy?
- How can I best prepare for sessions?
- What is your fee per session?
- What is your appointment cancellation policy?

You may also want to ask questions about the therapist's values, biases, and attitudes, if you believe the answers could affect your therapy. For example, relevant topics might include homosexuality, abortion or specific cultural or religious issues.

Be sure to discuss fees with your therapist up front. Most health insurance plans, including health maintenance organizations (HMOs), will cover treatment for anxiety disorders, mood disorders and ADD/ADHD. If you have health insurance, you may want to find out in advance if your policy covers outpatient treatment, whether a co-payment is required, and how many sessions are covered.

If you don't have insurance, the Health and Human Services division of your county government may offer mental health care at a public mental health facility that charges according to ability to pay. If you're on public assistance, you may be able to obtain care through your state Medicaid plan.

The Mental Health Parity Act requires large group self-funded group health plans and large group fully insured group health plans (such as employer-provided insurance) to provide certain benefits to those diagnosed with these disorders: Schizophrenia, Bipolar Disorder, Major Depressive Disorder, Schizoaffective Disorder, Panic Disorder, OCD, Autism, Anorexia/Bulimia.

Contact your state's insurance department to find out whether additional protections apply to your coverage, if you are in a fully insured group health plan or have individual market (non-employment based) health coverage.

During your intake or initial session with the therapist, ask yourself these questions:
- Do I feel reasonably comfortable with this therapist? Can I open up to this person?
- Is the therapist really listening to me? The therapist should be asking many questions during intake in order to get to know you, and get a handle on the issues you're dealing with.
- Has the therapist asked what outcome you're seeking from therapy and what changes you want to see in your life? If you don't have goals to shoot for, how will you know when you achieve them?
- Does the therapist's initial advice make sense to you? Does it help you?
- Do you see signs of therapist bias that might suggest that the therapist is not open to exploring treatment options? For example, is the therapist open only to natural remedies, or only to medication? If the therapist relies on unsubstantiated opinions about treatments instead of scientific research and their anecdotal impressions from other clients, be wary. Remember, you're looking for objective treatment advice and oversight. Your therapist will be your treatment guardian.
- Do you see signs that the therapist is mentally unhealthy? For example, she isn't good at setting boundaries, shares too much personal information about her own life.

To be effective, therapy sessions must offer a safe and supportive environment for you to explore past hurts and current hardships, work through your feelings, and work toward an optimistic and peaceful future.

Possibly you've heard horror stories about therapists.

Cold, pill-pushing money-grubbing psychiatrists...

She never returns my calls...

What to do First: Setting Treatment Goals

Takes weeks to get an appointment, then when I finally do, he bills me a week's salary and hands me a prescription without even talking to me. ...

While these stories are no doubt true in some cases, they feed stereotypes — black-and-white generalizations. And unfortunately, those stereotypes keep some people from seeking help when they need it. In every profession in the world, you'll find unempathetic, greedy or incompetent people who somehow managed to get a license. There are also bad lawyers and bad teachers and bad car mechanics out there. But there are many good lawyers and good teachers and good car mechanics.

What you should know is that there are many caring and competent therapists in the world. Many therapists intentionally chose their career because they wanted to help people. And there is a therapist out there who can help you, no matter what your problems are. You just need to do your homework and trust your instincts. Challenge the stereotypes.

4
What to do Next: Working with Your Therapist

Therapy has one important advantage over all pharmaceutical and natural medicines: Therapy has no side effects, other than the temporary discomfort you may experience as you confront your problems, face your fears, and work through past hurts and current problems.

But by now, you've probably realized that avoiding your problems doesn't make them go away. You can't go around them, you can't ignore them — you have to work through problems in order to move forward to a healthy future.

That's what therapy is for.

What Can Therapy Do For You?

Here's a general overview of how therapy can help you...

- Pinpoint the issues that contribute to your distress, and help you understand which aspects of those problems you may be able to solve or improve. Therapy can provide relief for the person suffering. A trained therapist can help you set realistic goals that will improve your emotional well-being. Therapists also help clients identify how they have successfully dealt with similar situations in the past and use these experiences to develop strategies that may work in the future.
- Identify negative or distorted thinking patterns that contribute to feelings of hopelessness and helplessness. For example, depressed people may take things personally or over-generalize; that is, to view circumstances in terms of "always" or "never." Therapy can help people incorporate a more balanced and realistic view of life and put their problems in perspective.
- People need relationships. Therapy provides a mirror of a healthy relationship which people can internalize and take out into the world to create healthy long-term relationships. A therapist can also teach you how to love yourself. And when we

love ourselves, we are more capable of loving others.
- Help people regain a sense of control and pleasure in life. People who are suffering from mental illness usually stop doing the things that used to give them great pleasure and enjoyment. Therapy helps them see that they have choices, and teaches people how to gradually incorporate enjoyable, fulfilling activities back into their lives.
- Learn how to cope with life's challenges and build emotional resilience that will see you through future challenges.

What to Expect From Your Therapist

In general, a therapist's immediate goals are to:
1. Assess danger; determine whether you're likely to injure yourself or others. Provide a safe environment for the person; if the person is suicidal or violent, hospitalization in a psychiatric institution for observation might be necessary.
2. Conduct an assessment and make a diagnosis
3. Provide honest, objective information about treatment options
4. Develop an appropriate treatment recommendation: Determine whether therapy is necessary, whether medication is required immediately or whether your symptoms are mild enough to consider using natural treatments. Therapists are not trained to make any specific recommendations regarding natural treatments or medication. They can, however, refer you to a psychiatrist or naturopath for further help.

During the initial intake, your therapist will request a complete history of your symptoms:
- When they started; when they began
- How long you've had these symptoms
- How severe they are; including, for example, whether you've had thoughts about harming yourself or someone else
- Whether you've had these symptoms before and whether you received treatment. If you've been previously diagnosed with a psychological disorder and received therapy, be sure and tell your therapist. Be specific: What was the type of therapy?

How often did you attend sessions? Was therapy useful? In what way was it useful or not useful? If you were taking medication or using natural treatments, give the details: What was the medication and dosage at start of treatment? Was the dosage changed during treatment? What were the side effects? Did the treatment help?

Your therapist should also ask questions about alcohol and drug use to help ensure an accurate diagnosis.

Two frequent causes of misdiagnosis are:
1. Focusing on the person's anxiety, alcoholism, or psychotic symptoms and ignoring underlying symptoms of depression or dysthymia. Good diagnosticians always look for a mood disorder first, even if the chief complaint is something else.
2. Diagnosing depression and failing to notice the presence of substance abuse or another disorder, (e.g., an anxiety disorder or personality disorder). Good diagnosticians never assume that a mood disorder is the person's only disorder.

Genetics play a critical role in increasing the risk for certain disorders, so your therapist will also want to know if other family members have suffered from mental illnesses and, if they were treated, what treatments they received and whether or not they were effective.

To ensure an accurate diagnosis, a thorough neuropsychological assessment may be necessary. Examples of tests include: Beck Depression Inventory, Beck Anxiety Inventory, Rorschach test, Millon Clinical Multiaxial Inventory, Myers-Briggs Personality Test and Minnesota Multiphasic Personality Inventory.

What are the Most Effective Forms of Therapy Used Today?

A therapist's theoretical orientation is an important aspect to consider when choosing a therapist. Orientation refers to the methods and theories therapists use during therapy. A method or theory represents a particular school of thought about what approach is likely to produce the best outcome. There are many therapeutic theories, and, in practice, most therapists employ more than one. Many therapists are 'eclectic' and draw from different theories as they tailor their treatment plan to the specific clients' needs.

Let's explore the psychological theories that are most commonly used to treat depression.

Cognitive-Behavioral Therapy (CBT)

A typical course of Cognitive-Behavioral therapy (CBT) consists of 12 to 20 one-hour therapy sessions. CBT focuses on the connection between thoughts, feelings and behavior.

Our thoughts, feelings and behaviors are inextricably bound: what we think and feel influences what we do. Cognitive-Behavioral therapy helps us identify distorted thoughts and perceptions that lead to self-damaging and relationship-damaging behaviors. Once you can recognize distorted perceptions, it becomes easier to break bad habits and stop reacting to situations in destructive ways. In other words, by altering your beliefs and thought processes behind the damaging behavior, you are freed up to recognize unhealthy patterns and make healthier choices.

A cognitive-behavioral therapist helps you learn to recognize distorted thinking, challenge distortions, and alter the thought process that's creating and perpetuating your symptoms. You'll learn how to change the negative expectations, assumptions and beliefs that are damaging your self-image, relationships and your health.

CBT is a process of learning, exploring and testing that helps you acquire new coping strategies, as well as enhanced awareness, introspection and evaluation skills. CBT helps you process and control future thoughts and feelings, which ultimately reduces your reliance on therapy, and reduces the likelihood of relapse.

Many people who are depressed can become paralyzed by their negative thoughts and develop avoidance behaviors such as staying in bed, overeating, or watching TV.

One healthy alternative, for example, is keeping a journal and jotting down negative thoughts. Often it's helpful to write, then set aside the journal and distract yourself in a mentally healthy way (e.g., exercise or call a friend). Come back and read what you wrote, and you may find that you're able to view your thoughts objectively, as if from an outsider's perspective.

Another simple behavioral modification technique is to make a list of positive, healthy behaviors. The next time you feel depressed, choose one of those positive behaviors, instead of crawling into bed with a spoon and a gallon of cookie dough ice cream. For example, call a friend, take a brisk walk, pet an animal or take a shower. Such simple distractions become positive, soothing behaviors, rather than merely passive acts. Performing a positive behavior, such as calling a friend, tends to increase your positive thoughts: I have friends who care about me.

Faulty, negative thinking tends to fall into patterns... do any of these patterns sound familiar?
1. Filtering: A tendency to look for the threats in a situation, rather than viewing the situation as a challenge or opportunity. Magnifying the negative details, but filtering out the positive aspects.
2. Polarized or Black-and-White Thinking: Things are either black or white, good or bad. If you're not perfect, you must be a failure. There's no middle ground; coming in second is not good enough: She hates me because I disagreed with her.

Black-and-white thinkers tend to use language like "always" and "never," polar opposites that are characteristic of a person who views the world in terms of extremes. Developmental psychologists refer to black-and-white thinking as "primitive" because it's characteristic of children. When we're young and first learning language, we express our thoughts in black and white terms because we haven't yet realized that the world is full of gray subtleties. A child, for example, who feels unloved assumes that she must be hated; she can't understand how love and hate can coexist together, or reconcile feelings that fall in between. When feeling stressed and emotionally overwhelmed, some adults slip into this kind of primitive thinking — regressing to the way they saw the world when they were children.

"When I became a parent, I was paralyzed by all of the theories.

What to do Next: Working with Your Therapist

Sleep with your baby/ put your baby in a crib. Nurse on demand/ feed your baby on a schedule. These parenting strategies were polar opposites, yet each claimed to be THE right strategy. And each had the research data and anecdotal evidence to support their claims. Who was "right?"

Neither. Both. What I learned was that I had to find the right parenting style for me and my baby. My personality and temperament are unique as is my baby's. What works for me may not work for everyone else, and vice versa. I did my research and set off on my own. I learned to trust my own instincts about what was "right" for me and my baby.

In other words, I grew up. No more black-and-white decisions. Every day, I make choices for my baby and myself that fall, happily, into the 'grey.'"

3. Catastrophizing: Always expecting disaster, exaggerating stress, making mountains out of molehills. Descriptions of events tend to include language such as "terrible" or "awful", e.g., I can't stand it! It's the end of the world! My life is ruined!
4. Personalization: A tendency to think that everything people do or say is a reaction to you. Comparing yourself to others, trying to determine who's smarter, better looking, e.g., He's got all the talent. Why are they staring at me? What's wrong with me?
5. Blaming Others: A tendency to blame others for your woes when things don't go as you wish, e.g., My husband made me do it. It's my boss's fault I didn't finish the report in time.
6. Rumination: People tend to dwell negatively on the past, e.g., If only I had…. Re-analyzing the past over and over again may not be constructive. You can't move forward while you remain stuck in the past. Obsessing and thinking about past mistakes over and over provokes chronic stress. Chronic stress provokes chronic rumination — a vicious cycle. Rumination, or churning negative feelings over and over again helps perpetuate chronic stress because it depletes your reservoir of motivation, perseverance, and problem-solving skills — all of which are required to facilitate positive change.

Psychodymanic Psychotherapy

Psychodynamic psychotherapy is a form of "depth psychology" that explores the subtle or unconscious aspects of the human psyche in order to reveal unconscious conflicts and the defense mechanisms that we use to avoid the unpleasant consequences of those conflicts. Many people will find that CBT is not effective in the long term unless it is combined with therapy that goes deeper. It is difficult to change thoughts and behaviors in the long term if your unconscious sabotages these changes. Once we become conscious rather than unconscious, we are able to make healthy choices around our thoughts and behaviors.

Our views and perceptions of our past experiences are organized around our interpersonal relationships, including — and especially — our early childhood experiences. Psychodynamic psychotherapy helps develop insightfulness, and develop your ability to trust those insights to solve problems and cope with stress.

Psychodynamic psychotherapy helps people understand the meaning behind their depressive symptoms and why they do what they do. The therapist and client will often talk about earlier life experiences to gain understanding of current life challenges. Previous difficult relationships will tend to play out with the therapist, which can help a client recognize how past relationships are affecting current ones.

Case Vignette

Lacy has been trying to be "popular" her entire life. She packs her days with endless social engagements and spends very little time alone with herself. She wonders why she always feels so drained and disconnected from herself. Therapy teaches her that the unconscious belief imposed on her by her family is: I must constantly be with other people to be happy. She has based her whole life on that belief. As her self-awareness grew through therapy, Lacy discovered she is an introvert and feels more energized spending time alone, balanced with a few close friends. As she changed her belief to "I am happy when I have enough space in my life for me to be alone," she began to have more energy and experience more joy.

Psychodynamic therapy can help people resolve long-term sources of their depression, such as bringing to light someone's painful emotions that are denied or repressed.

Object Relations Therapy

Object relations therapy emphasizes relationships as the primary motivational force in life, and assumes that family conflicts from early childhood help create a blueprint of how our "Self-system" will develop and maintain relationships later in life. Object relations-based psychotherapy can offer a deeper level of resolution by identifying and resolving the underlying causes of human conflict.

Object relations theory intuitively reflects certain truths about all human relationships — from the early relationships of infancy to friendships, marriages, and ultimately, the client-therapist relationship. "Objects" can be people (e.g., mother, spouse, friends) or things, such as transitional objects with which we form attachments. These objects and the developing child's relationship with them are incorporated into a Self, and ultimately become the building blocks of the Self-system.

We enter the world with a genetic blueprint that sets the stage for who we will become, but it's also our interactions with others throughout life that shape how our genetic predispositions will be expressed. Early in life, we have little sense of ourselves, or our identity. It's through our relationships with those around us that we 'absorb' parts of others (objects) and slowly build a Self-structure, which we eventually call a personality.

In childhood, we form relationships with our stuffed animals, toys and pets (transitional objects). Later in life, some of us form intense and even self-destructive relationships with food or alcohol, as well as with other people. The more traumatic our early self-object relations, the more rigid and resistant to change we become.

But the blueprint of self-structure can be modified. A therapist can help resolve old traumas and self-destructive relationship patterns, freeing us to mature and self-actualize. For example, we may distort our perception of potential spouses to conform to our internal image of an ideal mate; we may even try to manipulate them into conforming to our family template. But two years later, you may suddenly realize that you have no idea who your spouse really is, and you've reached a critical point in the relationship. You must now devote energy to breaking through the distortions and discovering each other, or go your separate ways.

Case Vignette

Joe has problems maintaining stable relationships. He has a tendency to get close to people too quickly, which results in many conflicts and break ups. Joe was not close to his parents growing up, so his desire for intimacy and attachment creates dependency in his relationships. He also has a tendency to become anxious in relationships; he craves closeness, but at the same time, finds it scary. He tries to get close to people, but then gets scared and pushes them away.

Since the therapist knows that Joe will relate to him the same way he does to others (the client-therapist relationship tends to mirror our other relationships in life), he gently suggests to Joe that it's a good idea to let relationships develop more slowly. Therapy is providing Joe with another "object" or person who can facilitate healing and growth around his inner conflicts and attachments. He can now be more conscious and capable of creating healthy relationships which in turn brings about more happiness.

Family Systems Theories

Your family experiences deeply affect who you are. We are forever connected to our families, even if we feel distant or disconnected from them. Families are interdependent: We connect to and react to the thoughts, feelings, and actions of other family members — almost as if we share the same "emotional skin." While families differ somewhat in the degree of interdependence, all family members need attention, approval, and support from each other and they react to the needs, expectations, and distress of other family members.

Family systems theories suggest that each family is an emotional unit; individuals do not exist in a vacuum, and cannot be fully understood in isolation from their families. Changes in one person's functioning are followed by reciprocal changes in the functioning of others.

In families, each member grows up with a role to play and rules to respect. Each family member was expected to respond to the others in certain ways, based on her role. Maintaining the same pattern of behaviors within a system may lead to balance in the family system, but may also lead to dysfunction.

For example, if a husband is depressed, the wife may be forced to take on some of his responsibilities to pick up the slack. While this role change may maintain stability in the relationship, it can also ultimately damage the equilibrium of the family dynamic. Over time, the wife may not be able to handle both of their responsibilities . The children may feel neglected because Mom doesn't have enough energy to go around. The children may also begin to carry a greater load than they should, which may establish patterns of caretaking and codependency that will show up in later relationships.

Interpersonal Psychotherapy (IPT)

Life is about relationships. We're all connected.

The goal of Interpersonal Psychotherapy (IPT), is to help people evaluate and improve interpersonal skills — how they relate to others, including family, friends and colleagues. For example, IPT treats Major Depression by focusing on interpersonal relationships and their contributions to mood abnormalities.

Even when mental illness is not caused by interpersonal events, it almost invariably ends up with an interpersonal component attached to it: The person's relationships are affected. People notice that the person is different somehow and tend to avoid him/her. They may tend to confide their observations to others, which can further alienate the mentally ill person. ("He's no fun anymore", "She's changed," "He's so moody and grumpy these days I don't want to be around him.")

IPT often focuses on events that are critical to the onset and/or perpetuation of mental health problems, such as:

Interpersonal disputes- where the person has had a fall-out with someone close to him (e.g., a family member) and the two are no longer speaking. Such disputes often extend to the wider family, who "take sides."

Conflict - where two people have an initial disagreement that turns into a running battle that lasts months or even years.

Role transitions — For example, the person has been asked to care for an elderly parent and none of the other siblings want to take responsibility. Or someone has been directed to take over a job role that doesn't suit him and isn't trained for; he feels frustrated but sees no way out due to financial commitments.

Complex bereavements- that extend beyond the normal bereavement period. Perhaps the person feels somehow responsible for the death of another person (e.g., a family member or co-worker).

Many psychotherapists believe that IPT can be an effective short-term treatment of depression. IPT also works well in conjunction with medications. Like Cognitive-Behavior Therapy, IPT typically follows a treatment course of 12 to 20-sessions.

Case Vignette

After Sara had her first child, she felt depressed and guilty and became convinced she wasn't a good mother. IPT helped Sara integrate her role as a mother with her sense of self and her other relationships — both at home and in the workplace. She attached to her new baby and learned how to be responsive to him. After a few months of therapy, her depression subsided.

How Much Therapy Do You Need?

Every client wants to know: How many therapy sessions will I need? There is, of course, no one right answer. Every client is different. Therapy must deal with the issues troubling you and help you manage your symptoms. For people who need more from a therapist than occasional treatment plan oversight, effective therapy will not be found in a 1-hour talk show, or a weekend workshop. It's almost never a quick-fix solution.

Some people require only a few sessions; others require therapy on a continuing basis for several years. On average, most clients who need ongoing therapy need it weekly for 3 – 6 months. But averages aren't worth much, when it comes to individual mental health. The number of therapy sessions required usually depends on the complexity of the issues you're dealing with and the severity of your symptoms.

The therapist should be able to estimate how much therapy you'll need within the first few sessions. What many people find, however, is that the initial sessions resolve the most pressing concerns, only to uncover deeper issues that must be dealt with.

The amount of therapy you need may be related to other treatments you're receiving. Medications usually show more dramatic results and work faster than therapy. On the other hand, practice statistics show that for most people, medications are no more effective than a 20- to 30-session course of psychotherapy. And for many problems, the rate of relapse is much higher for people who receive medication-only treatments than for those who receive psychotherapy.

As a rule, if the problem affects many areas of life and continues to occur, continuous therapy is probably necessary, either as an alternative to medication, or as a complementary treatment. Setbacks are not uncommon, and progress may be erratic, but if you continue to show improvement, the sessions are still providing benefit.

Many people who set an appointment with a therapist feel better immediately, just for having made an appointment. That's a good start. Sixty to 90 percent of clients who attend at least six regularly scheduled sessions find that they receive some benefit. You should begin to feel a sense of hopefulness, even if it's only tentative at first.

It may not be until you've attended 15 – 20 sessions that you begin to really notice symptom relief, e.g., that you feel less sad or depressed. After one year of treatment, most people find themselves relatively free of symptoms.

About half of those who remain in treatment for six months are helped substantially; about 80 percent are helped within a year.

Why do some people quit therapy too early?

People leave therapy for many reasons. Most people enter therapy with good intentions, but for some, motivation wanes.

The most common reasons people leave therapy are:
- Lack of education about the benefits of therapy
- They feel better in the short term, which leads them to believe they're "cured"
- They believe their symptoms are controllable without therapy
- Inconvenience; for example, work and family scheduling conflicts
- Therapy "hurts;" the client may not feel better immediately, and in fact, may feel worse while working through issues in the short term
- Cost of therapy sessions

A good therapist will educate you, support you during the rough times, and help you objectively evaluate your progress. Find a therapist you trust, and trust them to help you decide when you're ready to terminate therapy.

Which Treatment is Right For You?

The treatment options available to you will depend upon your diagnosis, symptom severity, and preferences. These may include psychotherapy, medications, natural remedies, or a combination therapy. Severe illnesses, particularly those that are chronic or recurrent, usually require a combination of treatments to achieve the best outcome.

In the upcoming chapters, you'll learn how to evaluate where you are now. You'll find specific information about available treatments, as well as research and clinical stories that may suggest the best treatment outcome for you.

5
Medication vs. Natural Treatments: Behind the Controversy

What are Psychotropic Medications?

The brain is a chemical factory. Every day, your brain produces its own chemicals, including those all-important neurotransmitters, such as serotonin, dopamine, norepinephrine and acetylcholine. Neurotransmitters are necessary for the transmission of nerve impulses across the synapses (junctions) between nerve cells, a process known as neurotransmission.

In order to synthesize and use these chemicals, the brain requires nutrients, such as amino acids, vitamins, and minerals. If the brain doesn't receive adequate amounts of these nutrient building blocks, neurotransmission problems result, and ultimately, mental and physical health disorders.

Psychotropic (also known as psychoactive) drugs are chemicals that act primarily upon the central nervous system, resulting in temporary changes in perception, mood, consciousness and behavior. Medications enter the brain through the bloodstream and alter the way that neurons (nerve cells) send, receive, and process information. Some drugs imitate natural neurotransmitters; for example, narcotic pain relievers mimic the effects of endorphins, the body's natural "feel-good" chemical. Others are similar enough to the brain's natural chemical messengers that they can trick neural receptors into activating nerve cells and triggering thoughts and behaviors.

The categories of psychotropic drugs include:
- Antidepressants — used to treat disorders such as depression and anxiety
- Stimulants — used to treat disorders such as Attention Deficit/ Hyperactivity Disorder, narcolepsy and appetite suppression
- Antipsychotics — used to treat psychosis and mania
- Mood stabilizers — used to treat bipolar disorders and

schizoaffective disorder
- Anxiolytics — used to treat anxiety disorders
- Depressants — hypnotics, sedatives and anesthetics

What are Natural Treatments and Complementary and Alternative Medicines?

In the arena of natural treatments, you'll often hear certain terms used interchangeably, and not always accurately. So, first, a few quick definitions...

The eclectic term natural treatments is used to distinguish a treatment from pharmaceutical medications or drugs. Natural treatments can include a wide variety of treatments — from herbal remedies (herbalism) and mineral and vitamin dietary supplements to natural procedures such as acupuncture, acupressure, hypnotherapy, massage, meditation, chiropractic or aromatherapy.

Complementary and alternative medicines (CAM) are typically also natural treatments, such as those mentioned above, but this, also, is an eclectic term that may include any treatment not considered "traditional" by the medical community.

Complementary medicine is used in conjunction with standard medical care; for example, taking an herbal remedy in addition to anti-anxiety medication to treat anxiety, or using acupuncture to help treat cancer side effects.

Alternative medicine is generally viewed as any treatment that's used in place of what's considered to be standard medical care; for example, treating depression with the herb St. John's Wort instead of Prozac, or treating heart disease with chelation therapy (which seeks to remove excess metals from the blood) instead of a standard cardiac care approach.

CAM practices are generally grouped into 4 major categories:
- biologically-based practices
- energy medicine
- manipulative and body-based practices
- mind-body medicine

Often, these categories overlap. A related treatment approach, integrative medicine, or holistic medicine, is a total approach to health care that involves the patient's mind, body, and spirit. A holistic approach combines standard medical treatments with CAM or natural treatment practices; for example, taking an omega-3 fatty acid supplement in addition to a prescription statin medication to reduce cholesterol, or in addition to prescription lithium for a bipolar disorder. You may also hear the term whole medical systems, which refers to complete systems of care that have evolved over time in different cultures and parts of the world. Whole medical systems may include practices from the four major CAM categories.

And just to set the record straight on the term *homeopathy*...

The term homeopathy comes from the Greek words homeo, meaning similar, and pathos, meaning suffering or disease. Homeopathy, also known as homeopathic medicine, is a whole medical system that seeks to stimulate the body's ability to heal itself by giving very small doses of highly diluted substances. This therapeutic method was developed by German physician Samuel Christian Hahnemann at the end of the 18th century.

The principle of similars ("like cures like") is a central homeopathic principle which means that a disease or disorder can be cured by a substance that produces similar symptoms in healthy people. Homeopathic remedies are derived from natural substances that come from plants, minerals, or animals. Common remedies include red onion, arnica (mountain herb), and stinging nettle plant.

The natural treatments we'll discuss in this book are not homeopathic remedies. In addition to procedures such as hypnotherapy, we'll cover herbal remedies (e.g., SAM-e) and dietary supplements (e.g, zinc) that have demonstrated significant benefit in treating mental health conditions. In general, these remedies are not highly diluted substances formulated to trigger similar symptoms in users, as are homeopathic remedies.

Confused? Don't worry about memorizing definitions. For the purposes of this book, we'll focus only on probing the issues surrounding whether and when specific psychotropic medications are necessary, and when mental health symptoms may respond to specific natural treatments.

Herbal Remedies and Dietary Supplements

Herbal therapies are beginning to gain widespread use as both primary and complementary treatments for anxiety, panic attacks, social anxiety, depression, bipolar disorder, ADD and ADHD. In fact, 1 in 3 American adults uses one or more complementary and alternative medicine (CAM) treatments.

In general, herbal therapies are used for chronic — rather than life-threatening — conditions, and most clinical studies suggest that they're most effective for mild to moderate symptoms, not severe symptoms.

Many herbal preparations require 4 to 8 weeks of consistent use to achieve significant results, though some produce improvement within a few short days.

The benefit of herbal treatments is always dependent on:
1. An accurate diagnosis
2. The quality standards of the remedy's ingredients and manufacturing process
3. Individual neurochemistry

What's All the Controversy About?

From medical doctors, medical organizations, and pharmaceutical manufacturers, you'll hear claims about scam artists looking to make a quick buck are bottling weeds and labeling their concoctions "Herbal Remedy." Some will tell you that herbal remedies and dietary supplements either have no effect or have a dangerous effect. They point out that these products are not strictly regulated by the Food and Drug Administration, and that different brands may contain different amounts of active ingredients. They'll tell you that clinical studies and clinical trials revealing the benefits of complementary and alternative remedies lack clinical validity. You'll even hear some in the medical community claim that "homeopathic practitioners are quacks."

All these things are true…for some products, some trials, some practitioners. But for others, they're patently false. Certainly all homeopathic practitioners are not quacks any more than all medical doctors are quacks. There are a number of conscientious and quality-conscious natural remedy manufacturers whose products have consistently demonstrated impressive results for some patients and offer great hope for a therapeutic future that has fewer psychotropics in it.

From natural and homeopathic practitioners, you'll hear claims that pharmaceutical companies are greedy and medical doctors are "prescription-happy," interested only in parting you from your money. They suggest that medical doctors will diagnose you on five minutes of history and send you out the door with a prescription. They'll tell you that psychotropic drugs have severe side effects, can be addictive, and can create other serious health problems.

All these things are true…for some doctors, some pharmaceutical manufacturers, some medications. But for others, they're patently false. There are many conscientious medical doctors who put away the prescription pad when they believe a non-pharmaceutical approach has a good chance of success. Many partner with psychotherapists and neuropsychiatrists or neuropsychologists to ensure that diagnoses are accurate, and that treatments cover all the bases.

Are natural remedies harmless?

Some providers of natural remedies will tell you that natural remedies are safe and have no side effects, which is not entirely true. "Natural" does not necessarily equate to "safe." While it's generally true that herbal remedies and dietary supplements (such as vitamins, minerals and whole food complexes) tend to have fewer and less severe side effects, some do not interact safely with prescription medicines or other dietary supplements. Some can, in fact, have harmful effects on organs such as the heart, liver or kidneys, especially when taken for lengthy periods of time in large quantities, or when taken by someone with certain coexisting medical conditions.

Many people prefer natural remedies because they view them as a more gentle form of medicine — medicine without the side effects. For the most part, this is true. But there are a few issues to be aware of.

First, high-quality herbal medicines and certain vitamin or mineral supplements can be pretty potent, especially when taken in large doses over a long period of time.

It's important to remember that herbs are medicines, too. A kinder, gentler form of medicine perhaps, but medicine nonetheless. As with all medicines, their effect on the body is cumulative. That's why they work, but also why the wrong herb can become toxic, or the right herb can become toxic if used to excess, or taken in conjunction with another remedy that it doesn't interact well with. Taking a vitamin or mineral supplement that you don't need can create an excess of that supplement in your body, and can throw your entire metabolism out of whack and create other disorders.

Second, natural remedies are virtually unregulated by the government. They're regulated in the same manner as nonprescription, over-the-counter (OTC) drugs. However, because natural products contain little or no pharmacologically active ingredients, they don't face the same safety and efficacy hurdles as prescription and new OTC drugs. The U.S. Food and Drug Administration (FDA) does require that natural remedies meet certain legal standards for strength, purity, and packaging. The labels on the remedies must include at least one major indication (i.e., medical problem to be treated), a list of ingredients, the dilution, and safety instructions.

The bottom line is that, in the natural remedies market, consumers have little assurance of safety or effectiveness. The marketplace is cluttered with fraudulent products from small players, and there's a vast quality difference among manufacturers. Manufacturing standards have been proposed but are not yet in force.

The quality and effectiveness of natural remedies depend on many factors; for example:
- Genetic strength of the seed
- Use of correct species
- Part of the plant used (e.g., leaves, stem, roots) and concentration
- Maturity of the plant at harvest
- Soil and air quality

- Elimination of bacterial contamination
- Climate and organoleptic factors (sensory properties of a particular chemical: taste, color, odor and feel)
- Storage and collection; post-harvest processing
- The compound bonding process used in manufacturing

Here are three proven manufacturers to consider and discuss with your therapist or a naturopath: MediHerb (MediHerb.com), Biotics (BioticsResearch.com), and Nature's Sunshine (NaturesSunshine.com).

What about the media's role in the controversy?

Healthcare receives considerable media attention these days, and media stories, as we all know, help shape public opinion. But a survey of media coverage suggests that most positive coverage is skewed toward pharmaceutical treatments; we're often led to believe that complementary and alternative medicine (CAM) "doesn't work" or doesn't offer a significant benefit. Overall, the tone of CAM stories is comparatively negative, even when the remedy under discussion shows remarkable results.

Strangely, research shows that the main theme of most stories on pharmaceutical clinical trials is the trial itself, whereas the theme of most herbal remedy clinical trials is around two-thirds focused on the trial itself and one-third focused on the medical conditions, the myriad of uses for the herb, and "the health risk associated with herbal remedies." (Bubela, Boon, Caulfield, 2005)

Also, CAM studies are comparatively underreported, and when they do get media attention, the quality of the analysis is generally lower; for example, they're often less likely to report the benefits derived, or what percentage of participants were benefited from these studies

Does the Media have a collective lack of faith in CAM? Or are they biased toward their pharmaceutical advertisers? Both are probably true, in some situations. It is true that the media rarely discloses conflicts of interest, such as whether a particular clinical trial was funded by a party with a vested interest in the results. Some trials are funded by the private sector (e.g., a pharmaceutical or herbal remedy manufacturer). Yes, the ugly truth is that clinical trial researchers sometimes have an agenda, and that agenda can bias the results. That's why it's important to "follow the money" when evaluating research studies and clinical trials.

You'll hear statistics on treatment odds and risk factors from both pharma and non-pharma advocates. As any researcher will tell you, every statistical association has only three possible explanations: bias, chance, or cause. In other words, either the researchers who constructed the study tainted the result with a hidden agenda or preconceived notions, the result was dumb luck, or the result does, in fact, prove the cause and effect hypothesis.

Even in the world of government and clinical academic research, yesterday's results sometimes end up being invalidated tomorrow as experimental bias or dumb luck. Sometimes, in the world of clinical research, as in the real world of treatment, it takes a few tries to get it right.

6
Which Treatments are Most Effective for Depressive Disorders?

"I grew up in the presence of melancholy, a feeling of loss over things that maybe I don't have or never had. It is a shadow for me. It's part of who I am. It is constantly there. I just know how, at this point, to sort of manage it."

"It's like a chemical thing in my family. My dad and I both have severe mood swings. I've had bouts of clinical depression and I've had bouts which are just garden-variety, or event-caused."
– Singer/musician Sheryl Crow, Ladies Home Journal, 2003

Most people who suffer from depression need treatment to get better. But 21st Century medical advances have given us new effective medications, psychotherapies and alternative natural treatments. The good news is that 80 percent of those who suffer from clinical depression can be successfully treated, and could feel better within a few short weeks. With early diagnosis, treatment and support, most people can conquer clinical depression and go on to live happy, productive lives.

Treatment options for depressive disorders depend on the severity and duration of symptoms, but may include medications, natural treatments or psychotherapy, or a combination of these treatments. Severe clinical depression, particularly when recurrent, usually requires a combination of treatments to achieve the best outcome.

Depression commonly co-occurs with other mental (e.g., alcohol abuse, anxiety disorders) or physical illnesses (e.g., cardiac conditions), which can often mask depressive symptoms or make them worse. Before treatment begins, it's important to determine whether the depressive symptoms are caused by another psychological disorder or by a physical problem, or both, in which case an evaluation by a primary care physician may be necessary.

But it's equally important for a mental health professional to conduct a psychological assessment. Unfortunately, depressive disorders are typically inaccurately diagnosed and undertreated by primary care physicians. In fact, a June 2003 Journal of the American Medical Association survey suggested that general practitioners still undertreat depression in a way that could be considered medical malpractice, if it were lung or liver disease.

Psychotherapy

Case Vignette

Harry Potter author J.K. Rowling finally sought professional help for depression when she found herself contemplating suicide in the aftermath of separation from her first husband. At the time, she was living in a cramped flat in Edinburgh with her baby daughter Jessica, unable to afford rent. It was there that she began writing the first Harry Potter book.

"Mid-twenties life circumstances were poor and I really plummeted," Rowling says. *"The thing that made me go for help was probably my daughter. She was something that earthed me, grounded me, and I thought, this isn't right, this can't be right, she cannot grow up with me in this state."*

Rowling's usual GP was away, and the replacement doctor dismissed her, saying, "If you ever feel a bit low, come speak to the practice nurse."

"We're talking suicidal thoughts here, we're not talking 'I'm a little bit miserable," Rowling has said of the experience. *Two weeks later, her regular GP, who had looked over the clinical notes called Rowling back in and referred her for counseling — cognitive-behavioral therapy. "She absolutely saved me because I don't think I would have had the guts to go and do it twice."*

"I have never been remotely ashamed of having been depressed — never," she said in an Edinburgh University interview. *What's to be ashamed of? I went through a really rough time and I am quite proud that I got out of that."*

– Source: Fox News, March 2008

Which Treatments are Most Effective for Depressive Disorders?

For many therapists, Cognitive-Behavior Therapy (CBT) is the treatment of choice for depression, though most therapists are eclectic, and will draw upon other therapeutic frameworks when necessary to optimize treatment for the individual. CBT helps people change negative or faulty thinking patterns and self-damaging behaviors that contribute to and perpetuate depression.

For some people with mild to moderate depression, CBT alone can be as effective as antidepressants for treating depression and helping prevent recurrence. For moderate to severe depression, CBT, paired with the right antidepressant medication is usually the most effective course of treatment.

Interpersonal therapy (IPT) can help people understand and work through troubled personal relationships that can cause depression, or make it worse.

Therapies that delve deeper into underlying issues like psychodynamic or object relations (See Chapter 3 on theories) can also be invaluable in resolving inner conflicts and in shedding light on unhealthy unconscious patterns.

What should you expect from therapy? Don't expect to simply "snap out of it" after the first session or two. Feeling better takes time. Your mood will improve gradually, not immediately. You'll feel a little better, day-by-day. As your depression responds to treatment, positive and optimistic thinking will replace the old negative, depressive thinking. Often, sleep and appetite will begin to improve before depressed mood lifts.

The following tips enhance any treatment for depression:
- Participate in activities that make you feel better — feel good. Go to a movie, a ballgame, a party. Participate in religious, social, or other activities.
- Exercise — get those feel-good endorphins up.
- Let your family and friends help you. Confide in someone; it feels better than being alone and secretive. Discuss your concerns with others who know you well and will have a more objective view of your situation.
- If you're feeling stressed, break large tasks into small ones, set priorities, and focus on doing what you can. Postpone major

decisions, if necessary. Avoid significant transitions, such as changing jobs, getting married, getting divorced.

How Family and Friends Can Help

The most important thing anyone can do for a depressed person is to encourage them to see a doctor or a mental health professional to obtain a diagnostic evaluation and treatment — make the appointment and drive them to the doctor yourself, if necessary.

The second most important thing is to offer emotional support. Help them understand that depression is a common illness, and that it's nothing to be ashamed of. Support always requires understanding, patience, affection, and encouragement.

Engage the depressed person in conversation, and listen carefully. Don't invalidate their feelings, but carefully point out distorted thinking. Invite them to social outings. If your invitation is refused, be gently insistent.

Encourage them to participate in activities that once gave pleasure, but don't push them too hard. Undertaking too much too soon or feeling pressured by too many demands can cause a depressed person to have an increased feeling of failure. Always offer hope. Don't expect the depressed person to "to snap out of it," or accuse them of laziness or "faking it." Keep reassuring them that, with time and help, they will feel better. Encourage them to stick with treatment until symptoms diminish, or to seek different treatment if there's no improvement.

"I've suffered from depression since my adolescence. Over the years, I've occasionally even had thoughts of harming myself. On some level, I knew these feelings weren't normal. But my family didn't talk about feelings, so I kept my thoughts to myself.

After I got married, my depression became so debilitating that my husband pushed me to go to therapy. It was the best decision I ever made. I learned to talk about my feelings, instead of stuffing them. I learned how to make new friends, which kept me from feeling so isolated. Friends have had a huge impact on my life. They support me when I'm down and encourage me to move forward. They help

Which Treatments are Most Effective for Depressive Disorders?

keep me from getting "stuck." I see the light at the end of the tunnel. Life has become worth living. And instead of thinking about ending my life, I'm setting goals and making plans for a bright future."

Natural Treatments

Herbal remedies commonly used to treat depression include: St. John's Wort, Omega-3, Rhodiola Rosea, Zinc, 5-HTP, and SAM-e.

St. John's Wort

St. Johns Wort is the most widely used herbal antidepressant in the market, and has shown significant benefits for many people with mild to moderate depression. St. John's Wort regulates mood by helping maintain balance among key neurotransmitters, including serotonin, norepinephrine, dopamine and GABA.

The effect of St. John's Wort can be quite powerful, especially over time. That's both good news and bad news...

It's good news for people who are able to replace pharmaceutical medications with this herb; bad news in that, for some, it can cause adverse reactions when taken with other medications and can reduce the effectiveness of certain medications (e.g., antidepressants and medications for HIV, heart conditions, seizures, certain cancers, oral contraceptives). Thus, St. John's Wort should be taken under a doctor's care.

SAM-e

SAM-e has been hugely popular in Europe for more than twenty years and many with mild to moderate depression have seen significant benefit. SAM-e is often taken in conjunction with other antidepressant medications. SAM-e however, is not for everyone. People who are severely depressed or suicidal should take Sam-e strictly under a doctor's supervision.

SAM-e functions similarly to SSRI antidepressant medications. SAM-e crosses through the blood-brain barrier and inhibits the reuptake of the mood-enhancing neurotransmitter serotonin, which increases the amount of serotonin available in the central nervous system.

Clinical studies show that SAM-e may take effect in as little as 7 days. 400 mgs daily (2 x 200 mgs) is the typical starting dose, which is often increased to 1600 mgs daily. Like pharmaceutical antidepressants, SAM-e is a long-term treatment that typically lasts at least four months, which means you shouldn't stop taking it abruptly after your depression has lifted.

Vitamins & Dietary Supplements

Nutritional supplements can help control depression, bipolar disorder, schizophrenia, anxiety disorders, eating disorders, attention deficit/hyperactivity disorders, addiction, and autism.

B Vitamins — B1, B3, B5, B6, B9 and B12

The B-complex of vitamins is essential for proper mental function and overall health. For some people, B-vitamin supplementation can help reduce symptoms of anxiety and depression, including fatigue, sleep difficulty, stress, nervousness, anxiety and depressive states.

For example, some people with depression have what's known as a genetic pyrrole disorder, which renders them severely deficient in vitamin B6. Pyrroles bind with vitamin B6 and ultimately with zinc, and this binding process depletes these nutrients. These people cannot efficiently create serotonin, since B6 is an important factor in the last step of serotonin synthesis. B6 supplementation can increase the amount of serotonin available to the brain.

Finnish studies have shown that depressed people on antidepressants who responded fully had higher levels of vitamin B12 in their blood at the beginning of treatment and extended up to six months later. Why? One explanation is that B12 is necessary for manufacturing mood-relevant neurotransmitters. Another theory is that vitamin B12 deficiency leads to the accumulation of the amino acid homocysteine, which has been linked to depression. Other related studies showed that people with high levels of folate (vitamin B9 found in leafy green vegetables) corresponded with a better outcome.

Omega-3

Omega-3 is a fatty acid found in seafood. Amino acids, such as those found in omega-3 fatty acids, are converted to neurotransmitters that reduce symptoms of depression, bipolar disorders and other mental health disorders.

The two active ingredients of omega-3 fish oil are EPA (eicosapentaenoic acid) and DHA (docosahexaenoic acid). EPA is considered to have the more significant therapeutic effect, so it's important to buy omega-3 that contains more EPA than DHA. In fact, a few studies on depression have suggested that DHA offers no beneficial effect whatsoever.

Magnesium

Magnesium, an alkaline earth metal, is the ninth most abundant element in the universe. and the 11th most abundant element in the human body. Its ions are essential to all living cells. Hundreds of enzymes require magnesium ion in order to function properly. Magnesium plays a major role in manipulating important biological polyphosphate compounds like ATP, DNA and RNA. Magnesium compounds are used medicinally as laxatives, antacids and used to stabilize abnormal nerve excitation and blood vessel spasms.

Low levels of magnesium in the bloodstream contribute to symptoms such as anxiety, hyper-emotionality, fatigue, headaches, insomnia, light-headedness, dizziness and "nervous fits." Magnesium has been shown to improve attention and reduce hyperactivity, hyperemotivity/aggressiveness.

Zinc

Zinc is an essential mineral that is found in almost every cell of the human body. Since depression has been directly connected with low blood-zinc levels in the body, zinc supplementation may provide antidepressant benefits.

Valerian Root (Valeriana officianlis)

Valerian Root is a calming agent that has a mild but direct sedative effect on the Central Nervous System (CNS), largely attributed to the valepotriate and sesquiterpene constituents of the root. Valerian Root promotes natural sleep after several weeks of use and can help reduce headaches, nervousness and symptoms of insomnia.

Gotu Kola

Gotu Kola, which has a calming effect on the body, has been used for centuries in Ayurvedic and traditional Chinese medicine. Its primary uses include improving circulation, and alleviating symptoms of depression, anxiety and ADHD.

Kava (Piper methysticum)

Kava (also known as Kava kava or kava pepper) is a member of the pepper family, native to the islands of the South Pacific. Kava's effects are often compared to that of pharmaceutical sedatives because of their unique action on the Central Nervous System (CNS). The body absorbs Kava very quickly, which helps ensure fast-acting natural calming and sedation effects. The initial effects people usually experience are a relaxed, more sociable state of mind and a heightening of the senses.

Side Effects. Kava has few side effects, the most noted of which was reported by the U.S. Food and Drug Administration (FDA): a potential risk of severe liver toxicity from the use of dietary supplements containing kava, though these cases of liver damage appear to be rare. People who have liver disease or deficiencies, or who are taking drugs that can affect the liver, should talk with their health care practitioner before using kava. Kava may interact with several drugs, including drugs used to treat Parkinson's disease.

Kava has also been associated with a few cases of dystonia (abnormal muscle spasm or involuntary muscle movements). Long-term and/or heavy use of kava may result in scaly, yellow skin. Avoid driving and operating heavy machinery while taking kava because Kava, a calmative, may cause drowsiness.

The dosage recommended by the U.S. National Institute of Mental Health is as follows:

Adults (18 years and older): Many doctors recommend starting with a low dose and gradually increasing intake over time. Typical doses range from 50 to 280 milligrams of kava lactones per day at bedtime. Sixty to 120 milligrams of kavapyrones have been taken daily. A dose of 50 to 100 milligrams taken by mouth has been used for up to two months. A dose of 100 milligrams of kava extract (WS 1490) has been taken three times daily. Doses as high as 800 milligrams daily of kava extract have been taken for short periods, but have not been studied over the long term and safety is not clear.

Scullcap (Scutellaria lateriflora)

Skullcap has a tranquilizing effect, and is often used to aid withdrawal from prescription tranquilizers and antidepressants. Skullcap should be used with caution, as long-term use can cause liver damage.

5-HTP (5-Hydroxytryptophan)

5-HTP is a naturally occurring amino acid. As a precursor to the neurotransmitter serotonin, 5-HTP has been shown to have mood-enhancing affects. 5-HTP is found in minute amount in foods such as cheese and poultry white meat.

Chromium

The mineral chromium is found in whole grains, mushrooms, liver, and brewer's yeast. Several studies have found that chromium — alone and when taken with antidepressants — is effective for treating mild to severe depression. A recent Duke University study, for example, found that 600 mcg of chromium picolinate reduced symptoms of depression, including a tendency to overeat. Chromium may act on insulin, which controls blood sugar and has been linked to depression and diabetes.

Other Natural Therapies and Extensions to Therapy

More and more, practitioners are experimenting with alternative treatments for depression. In general, these treatments tend to be most effective for mild to moderate depression. Many are also effective in combination therapies, since the odds of side effects or adverse interactions with medications or herbal medicines is extremely low.

Popular therapies include:
- Acupuncture may help balance blood flow throughout the body and resolve underlying energetic imbalances that may contribute to depression. Stimulating acupuncture points have been shown to release endorphins and enkephalins, evoking a calming, mood-

elevating effect.
- Acupressure & Massage can alleviate physical symptoms of depression, as well as the lethargy of mild depression. Acupressure is performed by applying steady, firm pressure on specific points throughout the body. According to Chinese medicine, depression can occur when you repress certain emotions, such as anger or guilt. In general, many of the studies conducted by The Touch Research Institute on the effects of massage therapy demonstrate a remarkable decrease in depressed moods, anxiety levels and stress hormones.
- Biofeedback (Neurotherapy): Receiving EEG (brainwave) feedback can reduce the severity of depression. Biofeedback is obtained by hooking the subject to an apparatus that measures physiological responses (such as heart rate, muscle tension, skin temperature and brain waves) while the subject focuses on a sensory cue that helps her relax. The goal of receiving biofeedback is to alter brainwave patterns through training. Biofeedback training is a systematized approach to learning how to relax and achieve more positive physiological responses. Refocusing energy in a self-empowering way enables the subject to have greater control over their autonomic nervous system reactions, including those triggered by stress (e.g., heart rate, blood pressure).
- Transcranial Magnetic Stimulation (rTMS): Some NIMH studies have shown that repetitive magnetic stimulation of the brain's left prefrontal cortex may help some depressed people in a similar fashion as electroconvulsive therapy (ECT), but without ECT's negative side effects.
- Meditation can be useful in relieving symptoms of mild depression. Meditation's calming effect helps ease tension, improve concentration, increase awareness of feelings, and relieve negativistic thoughts.
- Hypnotherapy can be effective in treating mild depression and anxiety, particularly when used as a relaxation technique. Clinical hypnotherapy can help people bring repressed memories to the surface in order to deal with them appropriately.
- Aromatherapy. Some research suggests that mild depression can be mitigated by applying certain essential oils on the skin

such as basil, bergamot, cedarwood, clary sage, frankincense, geranium, grapefruit, lavender, lemon, jasmine, myrrh, neroli, rose, sandalwood, spruce, orange, and ylang ylang.
- Chiropractic. Chiropractic involves manipulating or realigning the spine, joints and soft tissue to improve the body's structural integrity and nervous system, thus improving overall mental and physical health. In the process of relieving neuromusculoskeletal and visceral organ dysfunction, chiropractic treatments can help relieve the accompanying somatic symptoms of depression, such as insomnia or hypersomnia, fatigue and energy loss, and appetite dysregulation. Chiropractic manipulations also elevate mood and restore an overall sense of well-being.
- Phototherapy, also known as light therapy or light box therapy, can be effective in treating mood disorders, including both bipolar and unipolar depression, as well as SAD during problematic seasons (e.g., winter). In phototherapy, the eyes are directly exposed to full-spectrum bright light with a special light source, such as a light box or light visor.

    Phototherapy tends to provide quick results. Sessions usually occur in the morning which could last for 30 minutes up to 2 hours, depending on the strength of the light and the severity and responsiveness of symptoms. For some people with bipolar disorder, light therapy should only be used in short courses (to alleviate symptom severity or shorten a depressive episode) since it can trigger mania.

    Side effects may include eye-strain, headaches and insomnia. Scheduling only morning sessions can relieve insomnia, and all side effects may be reduced through dawn simulation, a technique in which light intensity is slowly increased to simulate a naturally rising sun.
- Exercise. Most therapists agree that physical exercise should be made a vital part of any depression therapy. Depression makes the body heavy and sluggish, and being heavy and sluggish exacerbates depression — another vicious cycle. Energetic, aerobic exercise stimulates neurotransmitters, and serves as an outlet for releasing negative emotions. Exercise produces endorphins, which are effectively an endogenous or natural drug

that energizes the body and mind and endows a sense of well-being. Physical fitness also boosts self-image, self-esteem and confidence.
- Nutrition. Diet can play a huge role in mood, energy and sense of well-being. For example, high-fiber foods boost energy and metabolism and the omega-3 fatty acids found in seafood help bolster mood. Some research suggests that high intake of caffeine, sugar and alcohol can contribute to depressed mood.

Pharmaceutical Treatments

More Diagnoses, More Prescriptions. We are identifying more people who have mental health disorders, and more people are receiving treatment. We've gotten much smarter about psychological disorders than we were fifty years ago and we've gotten much better at early diagnosis, intervention and treatment. We've made astonishing advances in terms of understanding fully what causes psychological disorders, and what goes wrong in the brain and the body when disorder takes hold of us.

The technology and information processing revolution of the past few decades has driven phenomenal medical breakthroughs. Sophisticated new tools allow us to investigate, diagnose and treat illnesses with greater certainty. Human genome research, coupled with sophisticated brain scan technologies such as Magnetic Resonance Imaging (MRI) and functional Magnetic Resonance Imaging (fMRI)), allow us to pinpoint the specific influences of genes, brain chemicals and brain structures on mental illnesses. They also help us develop targeted therapies, including — perhaps especially — drug treatments.

Yet, with all this technology and expertise…

Misdiagnosis and overprescription have become far too common.

Lately, Heather has been having trouble sleeping, experiencing fatigue and loss of appetite. She makes an appointment to see her family physician who tells her, "You're depressed," and writes a prescription for the antidepressant Zoloft. But what Heather's

Which Treatments are Most Effective for Depressive Disorders?

doctor doesn't realize is that Heather is actually an undiagnosed bipolar (someone who shifts between highs and lows); she needs to be taking a mood stabilizer medication in addition to antidepressant medication. The antidepressant he prescribed triggers a mood switch, and Heather experiences a manic episode. Heather has just become more difficult to treat.

Does this scenario sound familiar? More and more, primary care physicians have become the "first responders" for people who have mental health issues. The problem is, many primary care physicians have a tendency to prescribe medication without waiting for a mental health professional to conduct a thorough psychological assessment of the patient. Internists or general practitioners, who may not have the necessary training and experience to assess mental health problems, may informally diagnose a psychological disorder and treat it without doing an extensive evaluation. Primary care physicians may not be the best initial resource for psychological assessment and planning treatment especially when there are complex psychological issues involved.

And misdiagnosis almost always ensures misprescription.
The two drug categories most frequently overprescribed or incorrectly prescribed are antidepressants for Major Depression and stimulants for Attention-Deficit/Hyperactivity Disorder (AD/HD). Symptoms that are not in fact symptoms of depression can masquerade as depression. The same is true of AD/HD, as well as mania.

Medical doctors often rely on literature from pharmaceutical companies to stay abreast of what's going on in the field of mental health and to help them make diagnostic decisions. While pharmaceutical treatments have vastly improved the quality of countless lives, the bottom line is that drug companies have a vested interest in selling more drugs. Drug companies are not objective diagnosticians, and marketing literature is not clinical diagnostic criteria. No one should be diagnosed by a product manufacturer — pharmaceutical or natural.

Is there an upside to primary care physicians becoming more involved in evaluating and treating mental health conditions? Yes, absolutely. In the current healthcare insurance climate, the family physician simply is going to be the front-line doctor — the first physician to evaluate symptoms and determine whether a psychiatric referral is necessary.

Fortunately, modern primary care physicians are becoming more aware of psychological symptoms than ever before and are having a better understanding of the physical toll these symptoms are slowly taking on us. Hopefully, your doctor will also know that depression, for example, may not be "just a psychiatric illness." Depression is a behavioral manifestation of underlying pathophysiological processes that are linked to medical conditions they normally treat, such as cardiovascular disease, diabetes, cancer, and dementia. Depression shares common brain chemicals, gene proteins and neural pathways with these illnesses. And given enough time, the damage can accumulate everywhere.

But on the flip side, any treatment that reduces symptoms of a psychological disorder such as depression also helps protect us against other medical problems.

Although symptoms are not perfect clues to the underlying biological abnormalities from which they arise, they're often our best guides to the intricate workings of brain-mind and body. Psychological problems are classified under the broad umbrella of "mental health disorder," but mental disorders take a physical toll, as well. In fact, recurrent mental illness can become such a vicious cycle that the line between cause and effect blurs.

Is the psychological symptom causing the physical symptom? Or is the physical symptom causing the psychological symptom? Mental health problems typically present with both psychological (mind and emotions) and somatic (biological and physiological) symptoms.

Ultimately, there is no such thing as a "mind-body split." Our mental and physical states are inextricably bound. Psychological symptoms — what we think about — have just as much impact on our health as physical symptoms, and every diagnosis and treatment plan must consider both aspects.

Which Treatments are Most Effective for Depressive Disorders?

A neurobiological understanding of mental illnesses allows us to develop a personalized approach to treating all illnesses — whether mental or physical. An integrated mind-body view of mental illness as a complex of symptoms that are activated by abnormalities in the whole person — mind-brain, body, and spirit — will unify rather than splinter, empower rather than enfeeble. Consequently, we will be able to diagnose more efficiently, completely, and realistically, providing markedly improved treatment outcomes. And, an increased understanding of the bodily symptoms of mental illness means that physicians will be less likely to miss the underlying disorder or less likely to undertreat patients who present themselves with primarily physical complaints.

In a perfect world, physicians, who are trained to treat physical symptoms, work in conjunction with psychiatrists who are trained to treat brain chemistry, and also partner with therapists, who are trained to treat psychological symptoms. The ideal would be a team of multi-disciplined experts who could partner together to develop effective, combined, holistic treatment approaches to depression. This book is intended to help you develop an integrated mind-body approach to assessing symptoms and choosing the appropriate corresponding treatments.

Antidepressants

Antidepressant medications can help relieve symptoms of depression while the person simultaneously receives psychotherapy. For many people — especially those with severe symptoms, antidepressants are the key to restoring quality of life.

Many people are afraid to take antidepressants because they don't want to be on the medication for the rest of their lives. A good rule of thumb is to stay on your medication six to nine months after your symptoms have abated. Many people are able to stop medication at this point and be able to stay symptom free. Some people need medication long term, especially if they have a family history of depression, and the depression is more biochemical rather than situational.

Some people find that it's necessary to try different antidepressants and/or different dosage levels before finding the most effective medication or combination of medications. Antidepressants begin to alter brain chemistry with the very first dose. But a series of changes must first occur for antidepressants to achieve their full effect. Although some improvements can already be seen in the first couple of weeks, antidepressant medications must be taken regularly for three to four weeks (sometimes as long as eight weeks) before the full therapeutic effect occurs.

The three most common classes of antidepressants include the selective serotonin reuptake inhibitors (SSRIs) and two older classes: tricyclics and monoamine oxidase inhibitors (MAOIs). The SSRIs (and other newer medications that influence neurotransmitters such as dopamine or norepinephrine) generally have fewer side effects than tricyclics.

Selective Serotonin Reuptake Inhibitors (SSRIs)

One of the newest classes of antidepressants are SSRIs. This type of antidepressant alters the levels of the neurotransmitter serotonin in the brain, which, like other neurotransmitters, helps brain cells communicate with each other. Popular SSRIs include: Fluoxetine (Prozac), sertraline (Zoloft), escitalopram (Lexapro), paroxetine (Paxil), citalopram (Celexa), and bupropion (Wellbutrin).

SSRIs have fewer side effects than the previously-prescribed antidepressants, but they sometimes produce slight nausea or jitters especially when taken for the first time. These symptoms fade with time, though. Some people also experience sexual dysfunction with SSRIs, which may be resolved by adjusting the dosage or by switching to another SSRI.

Approximately 70 percent of people with Major Depression who are treated with SSRIs experience complete symptom relief. (Compton and Kotwicki, 2007)

How do SSRIs work? SSRIs decrease the reuptake of the mood-regulating neurotransmitter serotonin, which boosts the amount of serotonin available to the brain, and in the process, boosts confidence and self-esteem, restores a balanced and more optimistic outlook on life, and helps promote an inner resilience that helps a person cope with stress. When the immediate reuptake of serotonin is prevented, more of these precious brain chemicals remain available to do their intended work.

Generally, SSRIs take 4 to 8 weeks to reach maximum therapeutic effect; however, many people experience a positive mood change within a few days to a couple of weeks. For severe, recurrent depressives, long-term maintenance dosages may be required to prevent relapses.

Possible side effects of SSRIs may include: nausea, anxiety, insomnia, and erectile difficulties, such as delayed orgasm.

Serotonin-Norepinephrine Reuptake Inhibitors (SNRIs)

SNRIs, the newest class of antidepressants, inhibit the reuptake of the mood-regulating neurotransmitter serotonin and norepinephrine. SNRIs increase the concentrations of these chemicals in the brain, therefore increasing neurotransmission. Venlafaxine (Effexor), a phenylethylamine antidepressant, is perhaps the most widely prescribed SNRI.

Since SNRIs and SSRIs both act similarly, which is to elevate serotonin levels, they share many of the same side effects. SNRI side effects include appetite and weight loss, insomnia, drowsiness, dizziness, fatigue, headache, mydriasis (pupil dilation), nausea/vomiting, urinary retention and sexual dysfunction.

SNRIs' two common sexual side effects include diminished interest in sex (libido) and difficulty reaching climax (orgasm), though these side effects are typically somewhat milder with SNRIs than SSRIs.

CAUTION: SNRIs should be taken with caution in combination with St. John's wort as the combination can lead to the potentially fatal serotonin syndrome.

Tricyclics (TCAs)

Tricyclic antidepressants are older than SSRIs, and can be particularly effective for less severe depression, though they are associated with more noticeable side effects than SSRIs. As with SSRIs, the regimen starts with low doses that are gradually increased. Common tricyclics include: imipramine (Tofranil), clomipramine (Anafranil), Amitriptylin (Elavil).

Possible side effects of TCAs may include: drowsiness and the slowing of thoughts, dry mouth, constipation, weight gain, rapid heart rate, low blood pressure, painful or difficult urination, erectile dysfunction, and blurred vision.

These side effects can often be corrected by changing the dosage or by switching to another tricyclic medication.

MAOIs

Monoamine oxidase inhibitors (MAOIs) are the oldest class of antidepressant medications and are still the best depression treatment for a small number of people. Popular MAOIs include phenelzine (Nardil), followed by tranylcypromine (Parnate), and isocarboxazid (Marplan). People who take MAOIs cannot eat certain foods and beverages (e.g., cheese, pickles and red wine) that contain tyramine, or take certain medications, including some types of birth control pills, pain relievers (such as Advil, Motrin, or Tylenol), cold and allergy medications, and herbal supplements. These substances can interact with MAOIs to cause dangerous increases in blood pressure, though new MAOI skin patches may help lessen these risks.

MAOIs can also react with SSRIs to produce a serious condition called "serotonin syndrome," which can cause confusion, hallucinations, increased sweating, muscle stiffness, seizures, changes in blood pressure or heart rhythm, and other potentially life-threatening conditions.

Other possible side effects of MAOIs include: Drowsiness and the slowing of thoughts, dry mouth, constipation, weight gain, rapid heart rate, low blood pressure, painful or difficult urination, erectile dysfunction, and blurred vision.

Anti-anxiety medications

Anti-anxiety medications are sometimes prescribed in conjunction with antidepressants, but they are not effective as a sole treatment for a depressive disorder. Stimulants, such as amphetamines, are also not effective antidepressants, but they're occasionally used under close supervision for depressed people who also have other psychiatric or medical conditions, such as ADHD.

Other possible side effects of depression medications

Triggering Bipolar Disorder It's important for the prescribing physician to rule out bipolar disorder in a patient before prescribing an antidepressant since antidepressants can trigger a sudden mood switch into mania in an individual who is bipolar. If someone has a history of mood swings and is placed on an antidepressant rather than a mood stabilizer, they may shift into rapid cycling, where their moods shift from high to low and their depression will be much more difficult to treat.

Are antidepressants addictive? No. Antidepressants are not considered to be habit-forming or addictive. But some people do experience withdrawal symptoms (also known as discontinuation syndrome) when they abruptly stop taking an antidepressant after an extended period — usually 6 weeks or longer.

Signs and symptoms of antidepressant withdrawal may include: Irritability, anxiety, sadness, insomnia, headaches, dizziness, fatigue, nausea.

The best way to reduce or eliminate antidepressant discontinuation symptoms is to taper off slowly, instead of quitting cold turkey. Some doctors say that a single 20 mg capsule of fluoxetine (Prozac) may relieve symptoms within hours. Fluxetine has a built-in tapering off period, due to its long half-life. For someone who's been taking a high dose of paroxetine (Paxil) or venlafaxine (Effexor), a second 20 mg of of fluoxetine may be needed.

Some people have successfully combatted withdrawal symptoms by switching to a SSRI (from tricyclics or MAOIs), or switching from a SSRI to venlafaxine (Effexor).

Benadryl (diphenhydramine), an over-the-counter allergy medication, has also been reported to help with discontinuation symptoms.

It's important to note that adjustment doesn't mean addiction. Addiction involves harmful, long-term chemical changes in the brain that lead to physical dependence and uncontrollable cravings. Antidepressants are simply designed to restore normal chemical balance in the brain.

Keep in mind that, after you stop taking an antidepressant, it can sometimes be difficult to differentiate between withdrawal symptoms and re-emergence of depression. Monitor your symptoms and keep your doctor informed about your observations.

Case Vignette

In a 2004 60 Minutes interview, actor Jim Carrey revealed that the inspiration for his funniness was "desperation." In his youth, Carrey had a sick mother. "I think she laid in bed and took a lot of pain pills. And I wanted to make her feel better. I used to go in there and do impressions of praying mantises, and weird things — whatever. I'd bounce off the walls and throw myself down the stairs to make her feel better."

At the age of 16, his family "hit the skids." "We were experiencing poverty at that point. We all got a job, the whole family had to work as security guards and janitors. And I just got angry. I was angry at the world for doing that to my father. I wanted to bash somebody's head in, basically."

Despite achieving early career success, Carrey continued to suffer from depression. "There are peaks, there are valleys. But they're all kind of carved and smoothed out, and it feels like a low level of despair you live in, where you're not getting any answers, but you're living OK. And you can smile at the office. You know? But it's a low level of despair.

"I was on Prozac for a long time. It may have helped me out of a jam for a little bit, but people stay on it forever. I had to get off at a certain point because I realized that, you know, everything's just OK. I rarely drink coffee. I'm very serious about no alcohol, no drugs. Life is too beautiful."

Psychiatric Side Effects

Alcohol and drug use. Antidepressant side effects may cause mild and, usually, temporary side effects or adverse effects in some people. These side effects are annoying, but typically not serious or life-threatening.

Alcohol and street drugs may reduce the effectiveness of antidepressants; however, people who don't have a history of alcohol abuse or dependence can generally drink a modest amount of alcohol with the newer antidepressants. But it's important to remember that alcohol is a depressant, and alcohol abuse nearly doubles the risk of Major Depression. Alcohol abuse tends to cause social, financial and legal problems that create stress, which also increases the risk of depression. And while the underlying genetic mechanisms are unclear, some research suggests that drinking may trigger the genetic marker for depression.

Suicide and suicidal ideation. Antidepressants can have unintended effects on adolescents and young adults up to age 24. The FDA has reported that 4 percent of younger people who take antidepressants experience suicidal thoughts or suicide attempts, though a comprehensive NIMH-funded review of pediatric trials conducted between 1988 and 2006 suggested that the benefits of antidepressant medications likely outweigh their risks to children and adolescents with severe depressive disorders.

People of all ages currently taking antidepressants should be closely monitored for signs of worsening depression, suicidal thinking or behavior, or any unusual changes in behavior such as sleeplessness, agitation, or withdrawal from normal social situations, especially during the initial weeks of treatment.

Physiological Side Effects

Type 2 Diabetes. Some studies have shown that the risk of type 2 diabetes nearly doubles for people who take tricyclic antidepressants (TCAs) and selective serotonin reuptake inhibitors (SSRIs) simultaneously. Given the increased risk of type 2 diabetes in people with depression, it's a good idea for people with depression — especially those taking more than one antidepressant — to get regular screenings for type 2 diabetes. Depression is also associated with low insulin sensitivity, and pharmaceutical treatment of depression is known to decrease insulin resistance.

Depression is wrapped up in many of the issues surrounding diabetes. Obesity, for example, is integrally related to diabetes and can perpetrate a vicious cycle. The more overweight people are, the more prone to depression they become and the more inactive they become, thus, the worse the depression. Approximately 30 percent of adults with diabetes also suffer from depression, associated with poor metabolic control, reduced quality of life, greater disability and lost productivity.

The bottom line is that people with type 2 diabetes are at increased risk for depression, and people with depression have an increased risk of developing type 2 diabetes. Therapy aimed at modifying the behavioral factors associated with depression may help prevent type 2 diabetes. And diabetes prevention strategies may significantly decrease the risk of developing depression.

Adverse reaction with breast cancer drug tamoxifen.

Breast cancer survivors who take antidepressants (including Prozac, Paxil and, to a lesser extent, Zoloft) while also taking the cancer prevention drug tamoxifen risk breast cancer recurrence. Tamoxifen reduces the odds of a breast cancer recurrence by about 50 percent.

Worrisome new studies show that interfering antidepressants can not only lower the amount of tamoxifen's active form in the bloodstream, but can virtually wipe out the benefit tamoxifen provides. However, not all antidepressants react adversely with tamoxifen, and not all women have the gene variation that appears to reduce tamoxifen's effectiveness.

Cardiovascular Side Effects.

New research suggests that depression may literally break your heart. Columbia University Medical Center researchers have discovered that relatively healthy women with severe depression and those who are taking antidepressants are at increased risk of cardiac events, including sudden cardiac death (SCD) and fatal coronary heart disease (CHD). There may be several explanations...

This risk seems to be more strongly associated with antidepressant use than with depressive symptoms. More research is necessary to determine whether antidepressant medications directly increase the risk of heart rhythm disorders. Most researchers are reluctant to pinpoint antidepressants as the direct cause of higher risk of SCD because the use of antidepressants is also a marker for worse depression; that is, the more severe a person's depression, the more likely it is that the person is taking antidepressants. Also, coronary heart disease risk factors such as high blood pressure, diabetes, elevated cholesterol, and smoking tend to be more common among women with severe depressive symptom.

Other explanations for the link between depression and SCD may include autonomic dysfunction, higher resting heart rates and reduced heart rate variability.

So far, research has not suggested any relationship between antidepressants and fatal CHD or nonfatal heart attack. Most doctors believe that the benefits of appropriately prescribed antidepressants outweigh the risk of sudden cardiac death.

Are antidepressants safe during pregnancy?

Many women experience depression during pregnancy, especially those with a prior history of depression. In fact, the majority of women with a history of depression will likely relapse during pregnancy if they stop taking their antidepressant medication either prior to conception, or early in the pregnancy. Depression during pregnancy puts both mother and baby at risk.

Unfortunately, antidepressants do pass across the placental barrier, potentially exposing the developing fetus to the medication. Some research has suggested that SSRIs during pregnancy are associated with miscarriages and birth defects, but most studies disagree.

Some studies have indicated that fetuses exposed to SSRIs during the third trimester may be born with "withdrawal" symptoms such as breathing problems, jitteriness, irritability, difficulty feeding, or hypoglycemia. In 2004, the FDA advised expectant mothers to gradually taper off SSRIs in the third trimester to avoid adverse effects on the baby. Adverse effects on the infant are generally mild and short-lived, and no deaths have been reported so far. But on the flip side, women who stop taking their antidepressant medication during pregnancy increase their risk for recurrence, and may put both themselves and their infant at risk.

These mixed results suggest that women and their doctors need to weigh the potential benefits against the risks of antidepressants to both mother and fetus. One common treatment approach is to taper the dose during the last month of pregnancy to minimize the newborn's withdrawal symptoms, then return to a full dose during the postpartum period when women are particularly vulnerable to depression.

Are antidepressants safe while breastfeeding?

Antidepressants are excreted in breast milk, usually in such small amounts that the drug doesn't even register in infant blood tests. Few problems arise among infants nursing from mothers who are taking antidepressants, but, as with antidepressant use during pregnancy, the risks and benefits should be carefully weighed.

Guide to Coping with Antidepressant Side Effects

Sexual dysfunction:
- Wait for a tolerance to the medication to develop
- Reduce the dosage, if possible
- Take a drug holiday — reduce or skip the antidepressant over a weekend or once a week
- Consider a medication that requires only a once-a-day dose and schedule sexual activity before taking that dose
- Switch to a different antidepressant with a lower reported incidence of sexual dysfunction, such as bupropion or mirtazapine
- Men may be able to add a medication such as Viagra to treat SSRI-induced sexual dysfunction

Nausea:
- Take antidepressants with food
- Try an antacid or bismuth subsalicylate (e.g., Pepto-Bismol)
- Eat smaller, more frequent meals
- Suck on sugarless hard candy
- Drink plenty of fluids (e.g., unsweetened fruit juice, cool water)
- Talk to your doctor about dosage adjustments or a slow-release form of the medication

Which Treatments are Most Effective for Depressive Disorders?

Increased appetite/weight gain:
- Eat healthy, nutritious foods; reduce sugar and fast food intake
- Exercise at least 30 minutes each day
- Talk to your doctor about switching medications

Fatigue and drowsiness:
- Take a brief daytime nap
- Exercise (e.g., walking)
- Avoid driving or operating machinery while fatigued
- Take medication 1 - 2 hours before bedtime

Insomnia:
- Take medication in the morning
- Avoid caffeinated food and drinks
- Exercise at least 4- 5 hours before bedtime
- Follow a relaxing bedtime routine
- Talk to your doctor about temporarily taking a bedtime sedative

Dry mouth:
- Sip water regularly or suck on ice chips
- Chew sugarless gum or suck on sugarless hard candy
- Make sure you're breathing through your nose, not your mouth
- Brush your teeth
- Talk to your doctor about saliva substitutes

Blurred vision:
- Get an eye exam to rule out other causes of eye problems
- Talk to your doctor about a dosage adjustment or about special eyedrops to relieve dryness

Constipation:
- Drink 6 - 8 glasses of water daily
- Eat high-fiber foods, such as fresh fruits and vegetables, brans and whole grains; take fiber supplements, if necessary
- Exercise regularly
- Consider stool softeners as a last resort

Dizziness:
- Rise slowly from sitting or squatting positions
- Use handrails, or assistive devices
- Avoid driving or operating machinery
- Avoid caffeine, tobacco and alcohol
- Drink plenty of fluids
- Take medication at bedtime

Agitation, anxiety or restlessness:
- Exercise vigorously and regularly (e.g., jogging, biking, aerobics)
- Practice deep-breathing exercises and muscle relaxation
- Consult your doctor about temporarily taking a relaxing medication

7
Developing Your Treatment Plan

Once You Have a Diagnosis…

New mind-body science has shown us that those exacting, rigorous diagnostic categories we've always relied on may not be as "real" as we once thought they were. Mental health disorders are not always discrete illnesses with hard and fast boundaries. Psychiatric diagnoses are useful for describing what bothers people. Diagnoses help doctors talk to each another and to patients in logical, straightforward ways. In the coming decades, we're likely to see the lines between "disorder" and "disease" blur as we continue to identify more neurobiological causes of mental conditions, and more mental causes of physical symptoms. And that's okay. What matters most is not the exactness of our disease names — these names can never fully reflect the underlying disease processes. What matters is that you identify all the actual symptoms you have and treat those until they're gone, or as close to gone as you can get them.

Any treatment that leads to the remission of symptoms (and is not illegal, immoral, or fattening) should be considered. Symptom remission is your first goal — your guiding star. And if you're approaching this goal, you're moving in the right direction, no matter what treatment you're employing. The goal of this book is not to dictate what combination of treatments will heal any one person. What mind-body science teaches us is that whatever therapeutic pathway you follow is the right one if it leads to symptomatic remission and a fully-experienced life.

Working With Your Therapist

Let's talk about how to apply what you've learned about the symptoms and treatments to you.

When weighing a particular treatment option, we want to know whether the treatment will result in improvement. But that's not all. We have deeper questions…

1. Will the treatment produce an improvement faster than what's expected to occur without treatment?
2. Will the treatment be more effective than simply having a therapist who cares and supports you?
3. Will the treatment enhance the effectiveness of your therapist?
4. Do you have particular characteristics that make you more responsive to some treatments and less responsive to others?
5. Is it possible that the treatment will work for you, even if you're someone for whom improvement would not ordinarily be expected?

For people with depression, especially those who experience chronic or recurrent symptoms, the disorder itself can become a chicken-or-egg conundrum. The line between cause and effect blurs so easily and it can become very difficult for people to sort things out for themselves. Are the psychological symptoms causing the physical symptoms, or are the physical symptoms causing the psychological symptoms? To make matters more complicated, the treatments themselves can make distinguishing cause from effect more difficult. Are your symptoms a treatment-triggered event, or is the treatment simply not working?

Emotions don't exist only in the mind — they manifest as whole body experiences. Your body and your mind constantly interact with each other, and the messages your body sends can either magnify or inhibit your emotions. The limbic system — the amygdala and the frontal lobes in the brain's cerebral cortex — coordinate and regulate these emotional feelings and bodily changes. For example, if you're anxious, your heart races, you feel jittery, and have a hard time sitting still. If you're depressed, you may feel fatigued, lose your appetite, or have trouble sleeping.

A therapist can provide the invaluable benefit of oversight — objective ongoing evaluation.

How We Discover What Works

When prescribing a course of treatment, clinicians tend to look at "average responses" or "standard responses" among a group of individuals with similar symptoms and characteristics. The "standard" is the best starting point. It reflects general practice wisdom and, more often than not, is the best treatment path. Most of the time, for most people, the standard works. But not always.

In a perfect world, the first treatment plan would work as intended, with no need for adjustment and no side effects. But the truth is, even with an accurate diagnosis and a thoughtful, thorough treatment approach, it's sometimes necessary to experiment with different treatments (and perhaps different dosages) to find the optimum treatment for your unique neurochemistry. Accepting that experimentation may be the only way to find out what works is the first step toward finding the right treatment.

If you're one of those people who needs to try different treatments, you may feel as if you're being treated like a lab rat — you may feel frustrated and angry. But instead of being angry at the prescribing physician, it may be helpful to view yourself as being in charge of the 'experiment…' You've hired a team of professionals to help you reach a diagnosis and pinpoint what will work best with your particular brain chemistry.

Just as no two snowflakes are exactly alike, no two humans are alike. Doctors must treat the person, not the symptoms. And that may be the single most important quality to look for in a doctor.

Guidelines for Developing the Treatment Plan

Consider using the following approach to develop your treatment plan…

1. First, you and your therapist should work together as a team to develop a treatment plan. The therapist should educate you on what to look for, including:
   - Realistic expectations for progress and change
   - How you should feel when the treatment is working
   - How you will feel if the treatment is not working

2. Rule out medical conditions. Your therapist can help you determine whether you need to see your primary care physician to rule out physiological or medical causes of symptoms. For example,

certain medications as well as medical conditions can cause symptoms that masquerade as depression (e.g., viral infection, thyroid disorder, or low testosterone level). Your physician may need to rule out these possible causes through interview, exams, and lab tests.

3. Present your Mood Charts (in Appendix) and family history to your therapist. Continue to monitor and evaluate your Mood Charts on an ongoing notice.

4. If your symptoms are mild to moderate, and you're being treated under the care and oversight of a therapist and/or naturopath, explore every natural option first to determine whether you may not require traditional medicine to get better.

5. If natural remedies don't provide significant benefit/symptom relief in three to six months, you'll know that you need medication. Use the mood chart to continue monitoring your moods. Get feedback from your therapist. Get feedback from family and friends who have an opportunity to observe your behavior frequently.

It's important to understand that no treatment — not therapy, medication, or natural remedies — will yield instant results. Having realistic expectations, a little bit of patience, and faith in the therapeutic process will keep you marching down a progressive path.

Often, people have resistances and biases that hold them back. For example, some enter therapy believing that all therapists are quacks. They're likely to be critical of the therapist from the start and evaluate their progress from that perspective. It's critical to be aware of any resistances or biases you may have and try to work through them. If you have resistance to therapy, natural treatments, or medication, it will be more difficult to hang in there when the going gets tough, and more difficult to objectively evaluate whether or not a treatment is working.

6. If it becomes clear that you need medication to get better, it's best not to resist and run the risk that your symptoms will become

more severe, thus much harder to treat. For practically every drug on the market, there's good news and bad news. It is true that psychotropics have potential side effects. But it's important to keep the issue of side effects in perspective...
A. Most side effects are not life-threatening unless you have certain medical conditions, which should preclude you as a candidate for that psychotropic in the first place.
B. Often the side effects will cease when your body gets used to the medication.
C. Often, side effects can be eliminated by adjusting the dosage or times that the medication is taken. Instead of simply stopping medication, talk to your psychiatrist first about your options.
D. If the side effects are ultimately intolerable, remember that you can always stop the medication. Most side effects will abate quickly.

7. Work hard to get the most out of therapy. There is one certainty about therapy: The benefits you get from it will be commensurate with how much you put into it. It's important to keep your therapist "in the loop" about how you feel and how you're responding to treatment. Communicating openly with your therapist about treatment options and your treatment concerns can dramatically impact the outcome.

Making psychotropic medications safe and effective

Medication must be prescribed by physicians, usually psychiatrists, who can either offer psychotherapy themselves or work as a team with psychologists, counselors or social workers who provide therapy.

Most people are initially anxious about taking medication, in part because they don't know what to expect. This anxiety can actually create more symptoms and make it more difficult to realistically assess the drug's effectiveness. Find a psychiatrist you can trust, and let yourself trust them.

Knowing what to expect helps you adjust to treatment and increases the likelihood that you'll adhere to the treatment regimen and give yourself time to get better.

Ask your doctor:
- How long will it take for the medication to be effective?
- How does "effective" feel?
- What are the possible side effects?

Here's how you can help enhance the safety and effectiveness of your medications...

1. Provide a complete history. Before starting a new medication, tell your doctor about any other prescription medications, alternative therapies or over-the-counter medications you may be taking. If you've previously taken psychotropic medications, be sure and detail the medications and the results.

2. Monitor the effects. Medication works best — and safest — when treatment is regularly monitored by a physician who can change medications or adjust the dose if necessary. During treatment, don't hesitate to talk to your doctor about any problems or side effects that you may experience, even if you're not certain whether they're related to the medication.

Tip: Track your moods with the Mood Chart to help determine whether the medication is working.

3. Don't mix meds. Medications — whether prescribed, over-the-counter or borrowed —should never be mixed without consulting a doctor. Some medications, although safe when taken alone, can cause severe and dangerous side effects if taken in combination with others.

4. Don't stop taking the medication abruptly. Many people are tempted to stop medication too soon. They feel better and decide that they no longer need the medication, or they may feel it isn't helping. Often, people believe that they have "failed" at treatment or that the treatment didn't work for them when, in fact, the treatment was not given for an adequate length of time

or was administered incorrectly. It's important to keep taking medication until it has a chance to work.

Some medications are effective only if they're taken regularly, and symptoms may recur if the medication is stopped. Once you start taking medication, it's important not to stop taking it abruptly without talking to your doctor. Some drugs must be tapered off under the supervision of a doctor to prevent adverse reactions, and to give the body time to gradually adjust.

Some people stop medications too soon because they're experiencing unpleasant side effects. If the side effects are tolerable, continue on the medication for several weeks to see if the side effects subside. Side effects often fade once your body adjusts to the medication.

It may also be possible to eliminate side effects by adjusting the dosage and times you take the medication, or by switching medications. Sometimes it's necessary to try several treatments or a combination of treatments to find the one that works for you.

Making natural remedies safe and effective

- Buy products only from a reputable manufacturer. Here are three proven manufacturers to consider and discuss with your therapist or a naturopath: MediHerb (MediHerb.com), Biotics (BioticsResearch.com), and Nature's Sunshine (NaturesSunshine.com).
- Read the label. Where do the nutrients come from? Do you recognize any of the ingredients? Nutrients should be listed in a particular order with, in some cases, the source. In a quality, wholesome product, you should recognize and be able to pronounce most of the ingredients on the label.
- Use only under a doctor's supervision, in recommended doses.
- Don't mix herbs with pharmaceuticals, except under a doctor's supervision.
- Be mindful of exposure to sunlight (and possible burning), especially if you're fair-skinned.
- If you're pregnant or breast-feeding, don't take herbs without

consulting your doctor.
- Don't expect instant results. Many herbs require several weeks before their healing effects take hold.
- Keep your expectations realistic. Most herbs are best-suited for treating mild to moderate symptoms.

Psychoeducation and psychosocial support can help

None of us lives in a vacuum. Each day we exist in one or more social "contexts" (e.g., home environment, work environment, community group). Social treatments, such as therapy, address the social stressors that may be provoking a mental health problem; for example, people are less happy when they don't feel productive, or are financially distressed.

Psychoeducation can be a valuable social intervention. The family, friends and colleagues who comprise the mentally ill person's social support network often need to be educated about the person's disorder. Often, they're eager to help, but don't know how. The therapist can show them how. Education also goes a long way toward mitigating any stigma attached to the illness, which increases the likelihood that the person will adhere to treatment and avoid relapses.

Build a good support system in a way that feels comfortable to you. Some people benefit from joining support groups where they can share their problems and achievements with others. Some don't. Internet chat rooms can also be helpful for some, but internet advice should be followed with caution. Talking with family, trusted friends or a spiritual advisor can be helpful, but it's not a substitute for care and oversight by a trained therapist.

When talking to others — whether it's a friend or a support group — the action should be helpful, as long as you come up with an action plan, as opposed to just wallowing in your feelings.

Co-rumination — rehashing problems with others and dwelling on the negative feelings associated with the problem tends to create stronger feelings of closeness between friends and helps build high-quality friendships. But ostensibly supportive friendships based on a pattern of co-rumination can lead to increased symptoms of depression and anxiety, which in turn, leads to greater co-rumination. Studies show that teenage girls are especially susceptible to co-rumination, and are more likely than boys to take personal responsibility for failures.

How do I know if I need a second (or even third) opinion?

If this is your first time in therapy, it may be helpful to visit two or three different therapists to get a perspective of how different therapists work.

If you've been in therapy for a few months working toward realistic goals, yet you're not making progress toward the goal line, the treatment plan is probably not working. It may be time to see another therapist.

If you feel "stuck," it may be time to see another therapist. But this may also indicate that you need to work a little harder to help yourself get unstuck. Addressing your frustrations with your therapist will help you get a handle on whether the therapist is the problem or there's an issue that you need to do a little more work on.

If you're seeing a psychiatrist whose treatment plan is largely or solely focused on medication, it never hurts to get opinions from other psychiatrists who may be less focused on medication-only therapies.

If you've been on medication for 6 months or more and still haven't made progress, it's time to try a different medication and/or alternative treatment. If you've expressed your concerns to your therapist and the therapist has not offered an alternative, it's time to find a new therapist.

How do I know if I'm getting better?

Do you feel that you're getting better?
On a day-to-day basis, are you more stable and functional than you were before you entered therapy?
Are you achieving your treatment goals?

These are the litmus tests of whether you're getting better.

Here are some tips to help you evaluate your progress:
1. Ask others — your family, friends and therapist. Look for evidence other than your own feelings to corroborate the reality that you're getting better.

2. Review your initial goals and determine the extent to which they have been achieved.

3. Review any adjustments that you and your therapist made to the original goals and determine whether the revised goals have been reached.

4. If some goals have not been reached, determine whether these goals were unrealistic, or whether reaching them will just require more therapy and/or simply the passage of time (e.g., grieving a loss).

5. For unachieved goals, evaluate whether another form of therapy and/or a different medication or complementary and alternative medicine may yield better results.

Some goals are lifelong quests that require ongoing self-examination and self-modification, such as connecting to your subconscious thoughts and feelings, or improving a particular skill or craft. Such goals don't have a predefined 'termination date.' But you should have an awareness that you're continuously marking milestones on the path to recovery. You should feel more resilient when stressors arise and more capable of coping with your problems. When you feel good about yourself and your relationships, you may be ready to terminate therapy.

This may not be the final word you're hoping for, but the bottom line is this: The only person who can answer the question Am I getting better? is you. No amount of written goal achievement will be as rewarding or revealing as your intuitive awareness that you simply feel better and your symptoms are vanishing.

TIP: Use the Appendix Treatment Goals Worksheet (Pg. 176-179) to map out your treatment goals.

8
Resilience:
The Ultimate Stress Solution

Stress is a popular topic of conversation these days. It seems that someone is always talking about feeling stressed out, burned out, overwhelmed, or "losing it." If you've caught yourself saying (or even thinking) those words lately, you're not alone. A surprisingly 75 to 90 percent of all physician office visits are for stress-related ailments and complaints.

How stressed are you?
See if any of these symptoms seem familiar…
- You frequently catch yourself sighing
- You feel as if you're literally being pulled in ten directions all at once
- You make mistakes that are uncharacteristic of you…you forget appointments, forget to pay a bill
- You have a hard time concentrating or making decisions
- You don't sleep well at night, or you sleep too long
- You experience appetite changes — marked decrease or increase
- You're prone to sudden emotional outbursts; you often feel on edge, frustrated, easily annoyed, impatient
- Your alcohol intake increases; you drink more "to relax"
- You develop nervous habits or tics
- You don't get as much pleasure out of things you used to enjoy

If these symptoms sound familiar, yes — you're stressed.
Stress can sneak up on you. Stressors can pop up without warning, and sometimes, unfortunately, all at once. What qualifies as a "stressor?" Anything we consider to be threatening to us in some way, either physically or emotionally. Actual stress only occurs when we have doubts about our ability to deal with that stressor. Starting a new job, for example, can be stressful because we haven't yet convinced ourselves we can do the job. In other words, stress

becomes a problem when we have too much stress and not enough resources to cope with it.

Change is the culprit behind most stress. Whether that change is the birth of a baby or being served with divorce papers, adjusting to a new situation requires a lot of energy and good coping skills.

Most stressors you'll bump into throughout life fall into one of six basic categories:

Acute time-limited or brief stressors. A public speaking engagement or a job interview
- Stressful event sequences. A major disaster such as the death of a spouse or child or the U.S. terrorist attack of September 11, 2001 —events that create a series of new challenges, but will eventually end
- Chronic stressors. Pervasive, recurring demands that force you to change your role or behavior and have no clear endpoint; e.g., caring for a child with a permanent disability or coping with a chronically depressed spouse
- Distant stressors. Traumatic experiences that occurred in the distant past but still have emotional and cognitive consequences for you; e.g., childhood abuse
- Background stressors. Traffic jams, a baby wailing in the background while you're trying to conduct a phone conversation

We humans are so prone to stress that sometimes we even experience anticipatory stress — we get stressed before change even happens! When you find yourself worrying about something that hasn't even happened yet (and may never happen), try channeling that energy into anticipatory coping. Review similar past experiences to remind yourself of mistakes to avoid repeating and figure out what you can do to cope with this stressor more effectively than you have in the past. Worrying only increases your stress, but anticipatory coping helps you prepare for future stressful events.

When Does Stress Become Dangerous?

We all pay a heavy stress tax, whether we're aware of it or not. In one way or another, stress contributes to most psychological and physical health problems. If you have good coping skills, you can minimize the impact of stress on your health and relationships.

Stress becomes dangerous when it interferes with your ability for an extended period of time to live a normal life. For example, you may find yourself feeling "out of control" and have no idea how to fix even relatively minor problems. These feelings of helplessness can cause you to feel continually fatigued, unable to concentrate, or irritable.

Over time, chronic stress consumes more energy resources than your body can produce. Stress directly impacts your neuroendocrine stress pathways, changing your body's nervous system and hormone levels, and ultimately weakening your body's natural ability to cope with emotional stress and physical illness. Your hormones "burn out." This emotional burnout, coupled with feelings of despair, can easily trigger (or worsen existing) chronic depression.

Stress triggers your body's built-in response mechanisms; for example, have you ever found yourself sweating because you were about to miss a critical deadline? This reaction is caused by hormones that help our bodies cope with threats and uncertainties. Not entirely bad, right? That physiological reaction can kick you into gear and give you that extra boost of energy to save the day. Problem is, the longer your mind feels stressed, the longer your physiological reaction systems remain activated — your body gets stuck in crisis mode, which can lead to serious health problems.

If you're caring for someone with depression, it's important to be aware of how severe and prolonged stress can age you and take steps to manage your stress. Some studies, for instance, have shown that people who spend many years in the role of caregiver for severely ill or disabled family members look physically a decade older than their chronological age. Why? Because their bodies were no longer able to fully regenerate blood cells.

Stress and the mind-body connection

Ultimately, there is no such thing as a "mind-body split." Our mental states and physical states are inextricably bound. Our psychological or cognitive state of mind — what we think about

— has just as much impact on how we function every day as our physiological condition.

Handling stress in unhealthy ways (e.g., overeating or alcohol abuse) may alleviate symptoms of stress in the short term, but end up creating significant health problems over time, and, ironically, more stress.

While stress doesn't guarantee that you'll get sick, it certainly increases the risk. And stress can diminish your ability to recover from illness. People who have suffered heart attacks, for example, tend to have a much harder time bouncing back if they're also experiencing major stressors, such as financial worries or alcohol abuse. On the other hand, the ability to effectively cope with stress can significantly speed recovery from a heart attack.

We know that stress plays a major role in triggering and worsening cardiovascular disease, osteoporosis, inflammatory arthritis, type 2 diabetes, some (e.g., viral) cancers and infectious diseases. Stress literally attacks every cell in our bodies.

Every cell contains a tiny clock called a telomere, which shortens each time the cell divides. Short telomeres have been linked to diseases such as HIV, osteoporosis, heart disease and aging. The telomerase enzyme within each cell keeps immune cells young by preserving their telomere length — that is, their ability to keep dividing and generating new cells.

The stress hormone cortisol suppresses immune cells' ability to activate telomerase, which may explain why the cells in people under chronic stress have shorter telomeres. When the body is under stress, it boosts production of cortisol to support our "fight or flight" response. Elevated cortisone levels, however, wear down the immune system.

Short-term stress actually "revs up" the immune system — an adaptive response that prepares our bodies for injury or infection. But long-term or chronic stress causes too much wear and tear, and the system breaks down. Perhaps evolution made a tradeoff. When the emergency stress response is triggered, the body quickly mobilizes all its resources for action. Functions that are not on the emergency team temporarily shut down. When hormones are raging — preparing for battle — energy-consuming components of the immune system, such as white blood cell production, are temporarily suppressed.

The good news is that we can significantly impact our body's response to stress by, for instance, manufacturing more natural killer cells (called T-cells). These amazing fighting units have the ability to recognize and selectively kill cancer cells and virus-infected cells. Researchers have actually measured variations in T-cell activity based on subjects' interactions between stress and attitude. Dr. Steven Locke at Harvard Medical School questioned subjects about stressful events in their lives and their psychiatric symptoms of distress. He found that the T-cell activity level of the group with high stress and low symptoms was three times higher than those with high stress and high symptoms.

In other words, people under stress who know how to deal with it emotionally actually have greater immunity than people who have low stress levels but poor coping skills. We can live with daily stress. But in order to remain emotionally and physically healthy, we must be able to manage it.

How to Boost Your Stress Management Skills

Stress management is a learned behavior. That means you can start taking small steps today to boost your coping skills and improve your resilience factor.

When we're confronted with stress that threatens our stability, we appraise the situation to decide whether we can manage it or whether it's beyond our coping resources. Coping is any strategy you use to deal with a situation that strains or overwhelms your emotional or physical resources. For example, let's say that your boyfriend takes off for greener pastures... At first, you might feel angry and hurt, spend a couple of days alone — moping, even fantasizing about revenge, then you pick up the phone to call a friend and treat yourself to a nice evening on the town.

Different stressors require different coping strategies; grieving the loss of a child, for example, requires different coping strategies from handling a chronically nagging spouse. Coping strategies tend to fall into one of two categories: Problem-focused coping and emotion-focused coping.

In problem-focused coping, you deal directly with the stressor to change it or eliminate it; for example, you confront your husband directly about the long hours he's been working and the toll it's taking on the marriage. Problem-focused coping works best when the stressor is controllable; in other words, you can actually do something to change the situation — either change or eliminate the stressor.

With emotion-focused coping, you try to change the way you feel about the stressor. For example, when your boss is critical, you may not chew him out because you need to keep your job. But you might seek emotional support from empathetic friends and co-workers.

Technically, there's a third category of coping: avoidance coping. Common avoidance tactics include denial or pretending there's no problem, distraction, venting, and sedation or numbing (e.g., through drugs, alcohol, overeating). Unfortunately, this approach feeds the problem and creates more stress.

Men and women often process stress differently.

The "fight-or-flight" stress response in men is sometimes characterized as "tend-and-befriend" in women. Evolutionarily, males may have confronted a stressor either by overcoming or fleeing from it, whereas women may have responded by nurturing offspring and affiliating with social groups.

The difference in how men and women respond to stress is actually neurological. In fMRI studies of stress tests, men show increased activity in the right prefrontal cortex (analysis and decision-making), whereas women show increased activity in the limbic system — the emotional part of the brain. And the changes last longer in women, which may help explain why the rate of depression and anxiety disorders is twice as high in women.

Many stressors have both controllable and uncontrollable aspects. It's always helpful to break down the problem and identify what you can control and what you can't. For example, if someone you care about has a serious illness, you can seek the best possible medical care, but you can't change the diagnosis. So you must find ways to cope with your fear, anger and sadness.

Sometimes optimism can be a simple but effective cure. Maintaining an optimistic outlook reduces the risk of health problems and helps us recover from a major life stressor. Finnish workplace studies have found that the increase in sick days taken after a major life event was smaller for those who scored higher on optimism questionnaires than with those with low optimism scores. Sick leave is often considered to be an indicator of whether a person will retire early due to disability, as well as predict whether there's a higher likelihood of cardiovascular disease, cancer, alcohol-related illness and suicide.

Having pessimistic expectations increases our vulnerability to both mental and physical illness, which may be explained by the fact that pessimists tend to cope with stress by detaching themselves from emotional events, rather than actively engaging in problem-focused coping.

And maybe laughter is the best medicine, after all. Studies have shown humor to be a common denominator among people with good coping skills and high life satisfaction quotients. Students learn more from humorous teachers. Employees who work for a humorous or humor-appreciative boss are happier. People who are married to spouses with a great sense of humor are relatively happier.

You'll probably find that your coping strategies are drawn from a number of resources: external problem-solving skills, internal emotional skills, and social support from others.

TIP: If stress is getting the best of you, try keeping a Stress Journal for a few weeks. A Stress Journal preserves a record of the thoughts and events that caused stress and will help you identify patterns.

Here are some strategies that will help you monitor your stress levels and manage your stress more effectively:
- Understand how you experience stress. How do you know when you're stressed? First, you must learn to recognize when your own stress needle hits the red danger zone. We all experience stress differently. Notice how your thoughts and behaviors are different from times when you don't feel stressed.
- Identify your stressors. What events or situations trigger stressful feelings? Are they related to your spouse, children, friends,

family, health, financial decisions, work, or something intensely personal? Pinpointing your stressors helps you identify patterns. You might discover that much of your stress stems from issues that are easy to correct. Or you may find that you're letting brief situational stress get the best of you (e.g., getting stuck in a traffic jam) and you'll learn to relax, take a deep breath and accept things that you can't change.
- Monitor your moods and emotions. As you notice yourself feeling stressed, jot down notes about your moods, along with the thoughts, feelings or events that triggered your stress. Do you feel depressed? Anxious? Angry? Helpless? Resentful? Afraid?
- Recognize how you deal with stress. Determine whether you're using unhealthy behaviors to cope with stress. Is this a routine behavior, or is it specific to certain events or situations? Do you make unhealthy choices as a result of feeling rushed and overwhelmed, such as stopping for junk food while running errands or picking up the kids from school? This awareness can help you put things in perspective. Prioritize — make time for what's really important. Delegate responsibilities. Identify ways your family and friends can lessen your load so that you can take a break. Try and set aside the less important tasks.
- Find healthy ways to manage stress. Insert healthy, stress-reducing activities into your life... aerobic exercise, a short walk, or discussing your problems with friends and family. It's important to be aware that unhealthy behaviors develop over time, which is what makes them more difficult to change. Don't try to tackle too much at once. Focus on changing one stressor at a time, one behavior at a time.
- Walk away when you're angry. When you're feeling stressed, don't take it out on your spouse or kids. That's the most dangerous thing you can do and no good can come out of it. Count to 10 before you speak. Better yet, walk away. Engage in a physical activity to work off some steam. If you need to communicate your stress and anger to someone, do it when you're not stressed or angry.
- Reach out for support. Accepting help from supportive friends and family can improve your ability to persevere during stressful

times. If you continue to feel overwhelmed by stress, you should consider talking to a therapist who can help you manage your stress and change unhealthy behaviors.

How Resilient Are You?

We all experience stressful or even traumatic events in our lives, so why are some people able to cope with stress and trauma and others aren't? The answer may be resilience.

You may have heard the phrases "emotional resilience" and "psychological resilience" used interchangeably. Both translate to the same attribute: A capacity to adapt to and cope with stress, and to overcome adversity without becoming psychologically dysfunctional (such as slipping into a persistent negative mood or true clinical depression).

Think of resilience as your own personal coat of armor. Resilience is a kind of shield that helps you not only cope with the stresses of everyday life, but also protects you when you're confronted with stressful situations or traumatic events in the future.

How resilient are you? To help you assess your own resilience, take a look at the characteristics commonly associated with high-resilient individuals...

Characteristics of a Resilient Person:
- Can regain balance during hard times; recovers fast from traumatic experiences
- Can manage anxiety effectively and use it to solve problems
- Able to process through grief or loss without falling into depression
- Bolsters optimism, takes chances — embraces life, as opposed to engaging in harsh self-criticisms and dwelling on negative self-images
- Takes a "where there's a will, there's a way" attitude
- Tendency to view problems as opportunities, and making the most of those opportunities
- A deeply-rooted faith in a system of meaning; for example, the bond of marriage, spiritual, philosophical or psychological

- A healthy social support network (e.g., significant other, family, friends, work colleagues)
- Maintains better physical health
- Ability to adapt and competently handle a wide variety of problems
- Ability to persevere, navigate through the fallout after a crisis
- Possesses strong self-efficacy: Has confidence in their own ability to cope with adversity, whether independently or with assistance from others.

It's important to understand that resilience is a dynamic quality, not a permanent capacity. You can always make more. And you can never have too much.

People with lower resilience often find themselves worn down and adversely affected by life's stresses. The challenge remains that depression can lead someone with low resilience to negatively respond to life's challenges. For example, someone with clinical depression may feel depressed reading the list of "high- resilients" because they try to be optimistic and do the right things, but the depression feeds them a stream of negative thoughts. If you have discovered that you need natural treatments or medication, come back to this chapter to learn how to boost your resilience. It will be difficult to accomplish this if you are battling something chemical at the same time.

Certainly developing good problem-solving and decision-making skills can boost your resilience factor, but it's also important to build a strong social support system (e.g., family, friends, work colleagues, community organizations).

Strategies for Boosting Your Resilience Factor

When we think of resilient people, famous examples of high-resilients such as Nelson Mandela and Anne Frank may come to mind. But resilience can also be seen in ordinary people like you and me.

Resilient people tend to have these characteristics in common:
- Adaptive coping skills; they learn how to develop coping strategies and apply them to new future situations
- The capacity to make realistic plans, then take careful steps to carry them out
- A positive view of themselves, and confidence in their strengths and abilities
- Good communication and problem solving skills
- An ability to manage strong feelings and impulses

How do you develop these qualities in yourself? If you're dealing with a mood disorder, making changes can feel overwhelming, but here are some small steps you can take to boost your resilience factor:

Forge connections. Close, positive relationships with family members, friends and others are critical to boosting your resilience factor. Accept help from positive, supportive people who care about you and will listen to you. For example, you may find that talking to a therapist and being active in civic groups, faith-based organizations, or other community groups provides social support and instills you with optimism. And helping others in their time of need will also help you.

Avoid seeing crises as insurmountable problems. You can't always stop stressful events from happening, but you can change how you interpret and respond to these events. It's helpful to look beyond the present... focus on the ways in which future circumstances will be better. Pay attention to what makes you feel better, as you deal with trying situations, including small, seemingly insignificant subtleties that make you feel even a little bit better. Jot down a list of things you're thankful for. This may help you also put the current crisis in perspective.

Accept that change is an inevitable part of life. Accepting circumstances that cannot be changed will leave your mind free to focus on circumstances that you can change, and on strategies for changing the way you respond to adverse events. Some adverse situations may mean that certain goals are simply no longer realistically attainable. True coping skills help you get to the root of the problem and focus on changing what you can change and making peace with what you can't.

Take decisive action. When confronted with an adverse situation, take decisive action as soon as possible, instead of detaching from the situation, avoiding it, or denying that it's a problem.

Keep moving toward your goals. Develop realistic goals, and perform goal-oriented tasks regularly — even if you're only taking one small baby step at a time. (As any parent will tell you, babies eventually get where they're going, once they've made up their minds!) Don't try to tackle too much. Ask yourself: "What's one thing I know I can accomplish today that moves me closer to achieving my goal?"

Seek opportunities for growth. In times of adversity or loss, we learn something about ourselves, and there's usually an opportunity for growth. Going through tragedy and hardship can strengthen our relationships, deepen our spirituality, increase insight and our sense of self-worth, and allow us to walk away from the experience with a heightened appreciation for life.

Nurture a positive view of yourself. When you solve a problem, take a moment to congratulate and reward yourself, and do the same for others in your life. Part of building resilience is developing confidence in your ability to solve problems, and learning to trust your instincts.

Keep the problem in perspective. Even when you're facing painful events, try to view the stressful situation in a broader context. Take a long-term perspective. Avoid blowing any single event out of proportion. It may help to compare your problems to the serious problems around the world or even reflect on friends' challenges.

Maintain a hopeful outlook. Very often in life, we get what we expect to get. An optimistic outlook means that you will begin to expect good things to happen in your life. And guess what? You'll attract more good things into your life. Try visualizing what you want, rather than worrying about what you fear.

Don't forget to take care of yourself. Pay attention to your own needs and feelings. Exercise regularly. Engage in activities that you enjoy and find relaxing. Taking care of yourself helps keep your mind and body recharged and ready to deal with situations that will require resilience.

Identify strategies that strengthen your own personal resilience. Resilience strategies vary from person to person, so it's important to be aware of what works for you. For example, it might help you to write your deepest thoughts and feelings in a journal, particularly thoughts that are related to stressful events in your life. You may also find that prayer or meditation will help you feel spiritually grounded or building supportive connections renews your hope and optimism.

Building resilience will be different for everyone and takes time. The great news is that anyone can do it. We all have the capacity within us to become more resilient.

9
Improving Yourself

Take Steps Toward a Healthier You

Every therapist will tell you that the most effective therapies are those which revolve around client choice and participation. The most successful treatment outcomes belong to those who accept responsibility for getting better, actively participate in getting better, and help identify a variety of treatments that work for them. The more you can do to help yourself, the greater your odds of long-term success.

Make Time For You

Often, we're so focused on our roles and responsibilities in life that we forget to take care of ourselves. We don't put ourselves at the top of the list until we've already "crashed and burned." Self-care — making time to work on yourself — is a critical part of stress management and ultimately, reduction or elimination of symptoms.

No matter how busy your schedule is, carve out time for yourself every day. You will need to experiment to determine how much time you need to feel refreshed and centered. You will begin to notice an improvement in your mental outlook and a decrease in your body's stress response system. Mothers may have a difficult time with this exercise because they have such limited time to themselves. For anyone in a caretaking role, remember that if you feel good, you have more to give to those you love. Don't be afraid to ask for help from family and friends so that you can have the time you need to recharge.

Make a list of activities that nurture you and make you feel good and refer to that list when you are at a loss as to what to do. You may want to do nothing. Just being in the moment can be soothing and replenishing. Your list might include a bike ride, listening to music, or taking a bath. You may like to read, dance or pray. Think about the things you liked to do as a child. Maybe you've abandoned some of those things that made you smile and laugh when you were younger.

Let's talk about some effective therapeutic strategies that have no adverse interactions with other treatments, and anyone can do them, starting today...

Sleep

Contrary to popular myth, we do not "adapt" to getting less sleep than we need. The amount of sleep we need increases if we have been deprived of sleep. The importance of a good night's sleep to mental and physical health cannot be overemphasized. How much sleep do we need? Adults need 7 – 8 hours; adolescents, 9 – 10 hours; and babies, 16 – 18 hours.

Over time, sleep deprivation results in dramatically decreased cognitive, emotional, and overall physiological functioning, and can feed mental health conditions such as depression and anxiety. For example, sleep deprivation can make you seem — and feel — depressed (e.g., irritable, moody, apathetic, flat) and may raise up anxiety levels because you're less mentally and physically capable of coping with daily stressors.

During the deepest stages of early sleep, the body repairs and regenerates tissues, builds bones and muscles, and recharges the immune system. Thus, sleep deprivation decreases the body's immune response, so we become less able to ward off illness.

How "sleeping on it" helps decision-making and emotional health

Sleep is a smart, sophisticated process that helps the brain select what's important and consolidate or "burn in" memories of what we learned during the day. Fresh impressions of daily events are first stored as short-term memories in the hippocampus, then moved within hours (or days) — usually during deep, dreamless sleep — into an area in the cerebral cortex known as the neocortex, or "new bark," where they are stored in long-term memory.

Sleep improves the brain's ability to remember information and make decisions; thus, sleep deprivation impairs learning, memory and thought processes. Sleep strengthens procedural or "how to" memories (e.g., learning piano note sequences), as well as declarative or "what" memory (e.g., learning new words or concepts).

Sleep has a tremendous impact on our ability to properly assess a situation and make wise decisions. Sleep helps the brain selectively preserve and enhance those aspects of a memory that are of greatest emotional resonance, while at the same time diminishing the memory's neutral background details. In other words, of the hundreds of details that we process each day, sleep helps us remember what's most important and how we feel about those things so that we are better prepared to deal with them.

Sleep deprivation can impair our ability to properly integrate emotion and cognition (awareness perception, reasoning, judgment) into decision making, especially when the decision calls for a moral judgment. Studies have shown that sleep-deprived adults who are asked to judge 'appropriateness' in moral personal dilemmas have difficulty choosing a course of action, and are prone to making choices they wouldn't have in a rested state. You can see how loss of sleep can be critical to people whose occupations often require extended sleep loss and quick moral decisions under emotionally evocative circumstances (e.g., emergency medical services, military personnel, firemen and law enforcement).

What's your biological clock got to do with it?

We've all got rhythm — circadian rhythm, also known as our biological clock. Circadian rhythms are the body's intrinsic time-tracking system — they anticipate environmental changes and adapt to the appropriate time of day.

Maintaining a regular sleep cycle is a simple strategy that can dramatically improve mental and physical health. In other words, if you go to sleep each night at the same time and get up each morning at the same time, your biological clock won't be forced to reset itself again and again.

Why is your biological clock different from someone else's? Why are some of us morning people and some of us night owls? You can thank your genes for that. In fact, around 10 percent to 15 percent of our genes are regulated by circadian rhythms.

Our internal body-clock is regulated by a pair of genes: the gene (appropriately named) CLOCK and its partner BMAL1. The gene CLOCK acts as an enzyme whose job it is to modify the BMAL1 protein in a cell's DNA, which trips the switch on a whole genetic chain of events. If this amino-acid modification doesn't go off as planned, the switch can be thrown off, which can lead to a host of disorders, such as insomnia, depression, heart disease, cancer and neurodegenerative disorders.

Here are some final recommendations for sleeping well:
- Avoid caffeine, alcohol, sugar and other stimulants within 4 hours before bedtime; all can ultimately lead to sleep deprivation. Alcohol is not a sleep aid, and should not be used to make you relax.
- Alcohol, in fact, interferes with sleep's natural restorative processes which means you won't be fully restored when you wake up in the morning. Sleep deprivation actually magnifies alcohol's effects on the body, so a fatigued person who drinks will be more impaired than someone who is well-rested. And abstinence from chronic alcohol consumption sparks a burst of new brain cell growth; chronic alcohol consumption prevents growth of new neurons in the hippocampus, which impairs learning, memory and perception and prevents appropriate adaptive emotional responses.
While caffeine and other stimulants may temporarily overcome the effects of sleep deprivation, they can't boost energy for extended periods of time.
- Take time to wind down before going to bed. (That probably means no pre-bedtime thriller novels or movies and no TV news) Develop a bedtime routine that relaxes you; for example, drinking decaffeinated herb tea, listening to soothing music, reading, stretching, meditation, relaxation exercises, a hot shower, a soak in a warm tub.
- Exercise regularly, if possible. It will make you sleep better at night. It's best to exercise at least two hours before bedtime (preferably six), since strenuous exercise can be an energy

stimulator and may make it harder to for you to fall asleep.
- Don't go to bed stressing about that "mountain of work" you need to accomplish the next day or ruminating about something you "did wrong." If something that you can't do anything about at the moment is keeping you awake, write it down and remind yourself that you can deal with it tomorrow.

Exercise

Physical exercise should be made an important part of any treatment plan. Exercise has a direct relationship to mood: Physically inactive people have generally lower mood than active people. Depression, for example, makes your body feel heavy and sluggish, which only makes the depression worse — yet another one of depression's vicious cycles. But on the upside, taking a few laps around the block can do wonders for blowing off steam and can reduce depression and stress levels.

Energetic, aerobic exercise activities, such as running, biking, working out at the gym or playing sports, helps ensure a healthy mind and body and provides an outlet for releasing stress, anxiety and negative emotions. Exercise endows us with a sense of well-being by stimulating mood-related neurotransmitters, such as serotonin and dopamine, reduces the level of the stress hormone cortisol, and boosts feel-good endorphins that energize the mind and body. Endorphins are natural mood lifters that induce a calming effect when we're stressed. And physical fitness also boosts self-image and confidence, which boosts self-esteem — an effective antidote to negative, depressive thought patterns.

How much exercise do you need? Most research indicates that it takes at least 30 minutes of exercise a day for at least three to five days a week to significantly improve depression symptoms. But as little as 10 to 15 minutes a day can improve mood in the short term. And if nothing else, small bouts of exercise are a great way to get started, if you're having trouble getting motivated to do more.

If you're cynical about just how much exercise can impact your mental state, a recent Duke University study suggests just how powerful a mood-booster exercise can be. Researchers found that a brisk 30-minute walk or jog three times a week may be just as effective in relieving depression as any antidepressant medication.

Some researchers speculated that the reason exercise was considered the most beneficial treatment in this particular experiment was that the subjects were taking an active role in trying to get better, whereas taking a pill is a passive act. Either way, the results show that exercise is an important part of self-care. While it's important to point out that some people need medication to effectively treat their depression, this research can encourage all of us to make exercise a priority.

Some tips to help you develop the exercise program that's right for you:

- Talk to your physician or therapist about how exercise can fit into your overall treatment plan, and get recommendations on which activities might be most beneficial for you.
- Identify what you enjoy doing (and what you don't) and determine how you can fit this activity into your schedule. Doing something you enjoy will help you stick with it. For example, would you be more likely to do some gardening in the evening or go for a jog at dawn? Do you prefer taking a bike ride outside rather than going to the gym?
- Set reasonable goals. You don't have to start by jogging 100 miles a week. Start with a realistic, attainable goal and build up to your ideal goal. Tailor your plan to your own needs and abilities rather than setting unrealistic goals that will only add to your stress level.
- Try not to view exercise as a burden. If exercise is just another "should" in your life, not living up to the goal each day will eventually be associated with failure. View your exercise schedule as part of your treatment plan — like therapy sessions or medication, it's one of the tools that will help you get better. Search to find a type of exercise you like so it won't feel like a dreaded activity.
- Prepare for setbacks, obstacles and contingencies. For instance, if your daily exercise is walking or jogging, what happens when it rains for three days straight? Will you still exercise in the

rain? Or should you have an elliptical bike to provide an indoor alternative?
- Not sticking to the program? Exercise isn't always easy or fun, and you may be tempted to quit… and blame yourself. People with depression, for example, are especially likely to feel ashamed over perceived failures. Instead of being self-critical, figure out what's stopping you from exercising. For instance, if you feel self-conscious in a gym, exercise in the privacy of your own home. Do you stick to goals better if you have a partner? Find a friend to work out with. If you don't have extra money to spend on exercise gear, do something free — walk.

Give yourself credit for every step in the right direction, no matter how small. Skipping exercise one day doesn't mean you're a failure. Just try again the next day.

Go Outside and Play

Spending your days in climate-controlled, synthetic environments can have an adverse effect on how you feel and function. To improve mood and reduce depression, increase your exposure to sunlight — it's a terrific way to feel better. Eat lunch in a park. Take a walk after work. Just 30 minutes of being outside a day reprograms how you feel, and gets your patterns of sleep and wakefulness in sync with your body's natural circadian rhythms.

Nutrition

Giving your body the nutrients it needs helps prevent — and even treat — mental and physical illnesses. Diet, like sleep and exercise, directly impacts mood, cognition, energy and sense of well-being. Diet, in fact, is so important to mental health that it's worthy of being labeled a "natural treatment."

High-fiber foods, for example, boost metabolism and sustain energy. The omega-3 fatty acids found in fish help bolster mood, lower depression and improve cognition and attention. If you don't like to eat fish, you can take fish oil supplements.

Caffeine and sugar carbohydrates, on the other hand, spark a rapid rise in blood glucose or blood sugar levels, temporarily enhancing mood and boosting energy levels. But they soon turn on you, and send both energy and mood plummeting, which, of course, encourages more unhealthy cravings. (You can see the vicious cycle.)

Caffeine excites neurons and stimulates brain activity, which triggers the release of the hormone adrenaline. But after the first dose of caffeine wears off, the brain develops a craving for additional caffeine to recreate the effect, which is how caffeine addiction begins.

Sharp spikes and plummets in blood sugar feed symptoms of many psychological disorders — certainly depression, mania, anxiety and AD/HD. The temporary "rush" might be fun, but the ultimate result is lower mood, less energy, restlessness, agitation, anxiety, and an inability to focus, learn, remember, and think clearly.

Here are some simple brain-boosting nutrition tips that will help reduce symptoms of depression:

When you plan meals, focus on nutrition first, not cravings. Plan meals that don't take lots of time and energy to prepare before serving and you'll be less vulnerable to succumb to a craving for junk food.

Avoid synthetic dyes, preservatives and additives; they have no nutritional value. The body has to work harder to metabolize them, and they have been linked to irritability and restlessness (also inattention and hyperactivity in some studies).

Avoid soft drinks that contain sugar. Limit your intake of refined sugar, as well as other foods that contain sugar carbohydrates — they trigger blood sugar spikes which eventually plummet.

Choose foods made from whole grains (brown rice, whole wheat, oats, rye, barley) as opposed to those made with refined wheat flour. Eating several servings of whole grains each day helps prevent blood sugar from spiking and plummeting.

Be sure to eat your daily minimum requirement of protein (e.g., lean beef, pork, poultry, fish, eggs, beans, nuts, soy, and dairy products), especially at breakfast. Protein is involved in generating those all-important neurotransmitter chemicals that rule mood and cognitive processes such as attention and memory. Protein also helps prevent blood sugar spikes.

Eat fish more often. Fish, such as sardines, mackerel, trout, tuna and salmon, contain Omega-3 fatty acids which are essential for a healthy brain and nervous system. If you do not like eating fish, you can take a fish oil supplement.

Maintain an adequate level of vitamins and minerals each day; have a doctor test you, if necessary. Zinc, magnesium, iron and vitamin B6 all increase dopamine levels in the brain, which improves mood, increases alertness and attention, and reduces irritability and anxiety.

If you need a quick energy boost, don't head for the caffeine or sugar carbs. Eat a handful of nuts, dried fruit or yogurt. The high-fiber content in nuts makes you feel full longer, while low-glycemic fruit (e.g., berries) helps stabilize your blood sugar and slow energy store depletion. A source of protein like yogurt, which takes longer to digest, can also slow down your body's response to the carbohydrates.

Eat more fruits and vegetables, which contain the minerals, vitamins, enzymes and phytochemicals that your body needs for nerve and brain balance. You will get the most benefit by eating raw vegetables as cooking diminishes the nutritional value of these foods.

Drink plenty of water — ideally, 64 ounces per day. Water flushes toxins from your body and recharges your "electrical system." Water is an important companion to exercise. In addition to preventing dehydration, water flushes out lactic acid, the culprit behind muscle soreness.

The Plastic Brain

Just repeatedly thinking about doing something successfully can be as effective as the actual doing itself. You've heard the old expression "Practice makes perfect"? Studies of musicians and athletes, for example, have shown that repetition (rehearsal) solders in permanent optimized neuronal connections in specialized brain areas that are responsible for 'fine' movements of the hands. We owe this to brain plasticity or neuroplasticity.

Twenty years ago, we thought that once our neural networks

were wired, they were permanently hardwired — forever static. But it turns out, our brains are plastic, which can come in handy in the event of disease, injury or disorder. Neuroplasticity is the brain's ability to rewire itself, rerouting information processing functions to different brain areas and/or neural networks to compensate for damaged brain pathways and lost functions.

Over the long term, mental health conditions such as depression and anxiety slowly but surely rewire our brains. Numerous studies, for instance, have shown that the hippocampus of people who have been clinically depressed is smaller than the hippocampus of those who have never suffered a depressive episode. The hippocampus, you'll recall, is part of the limbic system, which rules emotion and motivation. The hippocampus also serves as our index or "map room" for memories.

But the good news is that we can undo the damage, it is reversible. Our plasticity potential allows our brains to be adaptive, flexible and responsive to change; it is the very essence of resilience. Plasticity evolves over time, which is why practice is so important.

The Desensitized Brain

Imagining a fear or anxiety while you're in a state of deep relaxation can help make those anxious feelings that might normally be associated with a particular stressful event begin to fade and eventually disappear — a phenomenon known as systematic desensitization.

Sometimes it's helpful to pinpoint the range and magnitude of fears that may be contributing to depression and anxiety. Here's a good reality check that helps put things in their proper perspective:

1. List the current situations in your life that bring about depression and anxiety.
2. Arrange these situations in decreasing order of their capacity to elicit depression and anxiety.
3. Put yourself in a state of relaxation. Imagine yourself successfully conquering the situation at the bottom of the list (the one that arouses the least anxiety). Keep re-imagining this situation until

you no longer experience tension while evoking the mental imagery of the situation.
4. Move on to the next highest fear-arouser on your list. Practice desensitizing yourself for a few minutes each day, knocking each item off the list, one by one.

Playing Defense

Sigmund Freud and his daughter Anna developed the theory of 'defense mechanisms' to describe the strategies that we adopt to cope with reality and maintain our self-worth. Defense mechanisms help protect the mind, self and ego from anxiety by preventing us from being fully aware of our unwanted or "unacceptable" thoughts, feelings and behaviors.

We all use defense mechanisms, even those of us who are psychologically healthy. But most of the time, we aren't aware that we're doing it. You could argue that defense mechanisms are actually helpful when they help us worry less about things that aren't worth worrying about, or that we can't do anything about, anyway. But too often, they distort our perception of reality and prevent us from taking action to improve our situation, and that's when they hurt us.

For example, a spouse in denial might pretend that she's happy in her marriage, smiling at her husband behind seething anger. The longer she avoids facing the problems in her marriage, the bigger they become. Her denial only makes her angrier, and does nothing to improve her marriage. Anger is not pretty. It's not fun to deal with. But once she faces the truth and becomes willing to discuss how angry and sad she feels with her husband, she is free — free to get the information and support she needs, free to focus on improving the marriage, and free to become healthy and whole.

Hopefully, the following summary of the most common defense mechanisms will help heighten your awareness of your own defenses.

Denial

Denial is the most well-known defense. You've mostly likely seen it at work in someone grieving... they may act as if nothing has happened, or appear to be unaffected by the death of a loved one. Drug addicts and alcoholics are also masters of denial, too; they can convince themselves and — may even convince others — that they don't have a problem. While denial may protect us from the emotional pain of reality in the short term, keeping it up consumes a great deal of psychic energy. And coping with our real feelings sooner, rather than later, saves us a great deal of pain in the long run.

Displacement

We've all experienced someone displacing their anger onto us. Displacement is the act of directing your anger from an anxiety-provoking situation at the safe person in your life. If you yell at your spouse for no reason, you may be displacing your anger from a conflict that you had with your boss earlier that day. Children often displace anger onto a parent when they have a problem with a peer or other adult that they haven't resolved.

Regression

Regression is reverting back to an earlier stage of childhood development when you're faced with unpleasant circumstances or feelings. For example, a 43-year-old woman might feel and act like she's 5 years old again when she's around her family of origin because they treat her like a child.

Compartmentalization

In compartmentalization, parts of the psyche are split off into compartments — separated in awareness from other parts — which allows us to behave in ways that are contrary to our accepted set of values. For example, someone may see themselves as honest, yet, they are stealing money from their employer. They may be able to unconsciously compartmentalize their acts of theft without guilt and be unaware of the obvious cognitive dissonance.

Projection

Projection occurs when someone attributes their unacceptable feelings to someone else; for example, an angry partner accuses a spouse of being angry or hostile, or you're in a bad mood but accuse someone else of being in a bad mood. Projection often occurs during therapy; a client may project their feelings of low self-worth and assume that the therapist just doesn't like them.

Reaction Formation

Reaction formation is doing or saying things that are the opposite of how we really feel because our true feelings are unacceptable. For example, someone who is very angry at a friend may act overly kind and generous towards the friend because they feel guilty about being angry; or a parent who doesn't want her child may become smothering and overprotective.

Rationalization

Rationalization is using conscious reasoning to explain away something painful in order to cope with the changing reality and anxiety it produces. Often, rationalization is a way of absolving ourselves of responsibility. For example, a woman makes a new friend who she thinks will be her best friend forever, idealizing the relationship. If this new friend disappoints her and doesn't want to be her friend anymore, she says, "I knew there was something wrong with her."

Sublimation

Sublimation is the act of channeling unacceptable impulses into more acceptable ones. For example, someone desiring sexual promiscuity may focus that energy on aerobic classes. Someone angry or violent may choose to take up boxing. Freud believed that sublimation showed maturity in that, through sublimation, people could live in society "appropriately."

Repression

Repression, a primitive first-line defense, allows us to push thoughts and memories out of conscious awareness, sometimes permanently. Unfortunately, these memories don't really disappear; they continue to influence the person's thoughts, feelings and behaviors. For example, a person who has repressed sexual abuse and doesn't work through those memories and feelings can have difficulty trusting others in relationships and experience difficulty in sexual relationships.

Dissociation

Dissociation is effectively a disintegration of the normally integrated functions of consciousness, memory, identity, and perception. A person may dissociate or detach themselves from reality or conscious awareness to avoid unpleasant memories and flashbacks of a traumatic experience such as abuse. We all dissociate a little bit; daydreaming, for example is dissociative. But at the extreme form, these dissociative episodes can result in conditions such as amnesia or cause a person to split into multiple selves (a dissociative identity disorder known as Multiple Personality Disorder).

You can see why, perhaps, the best defense is no defense at all. Often, once we face a painful memory or a fearful situation, the reality is not as bad as we feared. Ultimately, it is only through awareness that healing and healthy living can emerge. And the sooner you become aware of your defense mechanisms, the better off you'll be.

A therapist can be helpful when confronting and breaking down defenses. The therapist can provide support as you work through the unpleasant thoughts and feelings you may have been defending against.

Strategies for Good Emotional Health

Can you see negative patterns in your life that are making it difficult for you to be happy? Here are some practical changes everyone can make that will enhance emotional growth.

1. Take care of yourself. Take time to eat right, exercise, relax, spend time with people you enjoy, and do activities that you find pleasurable. When you're at your best, you can give the most to the relationships that are important to you.

2. Difficulties always present an opportunity for growth. Choose to find the positive things in life rather than focusing on the negative. Most people engage in affective misforecasting — we don't always feel as happy as we thought we would once we achieve a goal. We tend to pay more attention to disappointments than to experiences that exceed our expectations. When we feel better about an outcome than we anticipated we would, we take it for granted. But when something fails to meet our expectations, that is when we begin to notice and we start feeling worse than we thought we would.

3. Let go of the past. Be kind to yourself. Don't waste time and energy on things that don't benefit you. Forgive yourself and others. If you can't change it or have no control over it, let it go.

4. Be respectful and responsible. Don't get caught up in blaming other people. Do what's right for you, instead of worrying about others.

5. Acknowledge and reward yourself for your successes and accomplishments.

6. Develop one or two close relationships that allow you to be honest about your thoughts and feelings. Spending quality time with open, caring and sincere loved ones is nurturing — you'll gain support and encouragement. Emotionally healthy people create a good support system.

7. Remove yourself from hurtful or damaging situations. Walk away from a situation for awhile if it's getting out of control. Give yourself some space to problem-solve and develop a positive approach. Reach out for support, if necessary.

8. Talk positively to yourself. Don't beat up yourself with negative self-talk.

9. Be flexible; flexibility is part of resilience. Life never stays the same. Our circumstances never stay the same. We are always changing and growing. We have choices in how we respond to change and we may need to make adjustments in our lives in order to adapt in a healthy way. See the changes as an opportunity to grow and to learn new things.

10. Have a plan for the future. Develop long-range goals for yourself, and work on them one day at a time.

10
Science and the Effect of Genes on Depression

These days, it's popular to blame our genes for all our psychological problems, and when it comes to disorder and disease, certainly our genes are not blameless. But, do genes really seal our fate? Are we inevitably doomed (or blessed) to become our parents, with the exact same natural talents, intellectual abilities, diseases and disorders that they have? Absolutely not.

Genes don't guarantee your destiny, but they do have a say in who you become. Genes influence potential, possibility, probability. But so does environment, personality, culture, geography and experience.

In the nineteenth century, even the most educated people widely believed that biology is destiny. In the twentieth century, many psychologists viewed infants as blank slates to be written on by parents and teachers. Both theories, as it turns out, were oversimplifications. Neither was completely true nor completely false.

In the twenty-first century, the nature-versus-nurture debate is alive and well. Year after year, the best scientific minds and millions of research dollars are devoted to calculating how much our genes contribute to who we are and the degree to which we're molded by our environment. The answers are seldom black and white. And often, the answers raise new questions.

Sometimes we're asking the wrong questions. The useful nature-nurture questions revolve around the degree to which differences in a trait among a group of individuals are caused by differences in genes or by differences in their environments. When scientists study the relative influence of nature and nurture, they're trying to pinpoint how much of human nature is inherited — genetically. Heritability is the degree to which variation in a particular trait within a certain group comes from individual genetic differences.

Why are some people smarter than others? Why do some people have AD/HD and others don't? Why do some people who've "had

Science and the Effect of Genes on Depression

an easy life" develop depression and anxiety, while others who've endured hardship after hardship survive and even thrive? Nature-nurture studies can help us explain or predict differences between groups of people, but they don't necessarily help us predict why individuals do the things they do.

When we talk about "environment," it's important to remember that environment is influenced by culture — a particular system of shared ideas that shapes how we learn, think and behave. For instance, the fact that you're able to read and speak the English language is a result of your culture, not your genes. We're all genetically hard-wired with the capacity to learn multiple languages.

Our cultural experiences and beliefs influence what we consider to be appropriate, moral, or "normal" behavior, what motivates us, how we respond emotionally — even what feel guilty about. In many cultures, for example, it's not socially acceptable to seek help for psychological problems. In some cultures, people grow up with the belief that depression or anxiety is the devil attacking or possessing the human spirit; in the U.S., a clinician might view such a belief as delusional, psychotic.

Ultimately, we're the product of both nature and nurture: Our genetic inheritance gives us our biological potential. Our environment, including our culture, determines how we express that potential.

What are Genes and What Do They Do?

When sperm and egg unite, they create a new cell called a zygote. This zygote contains the full human complement of 23 paired chromosomes, with one member of each pair coming from each parent. The zygote grows up and becomes you. You've inherited 50 percent of your genes from your mother and the other 50 percent from your father, as did each of your siblings.

Every cell in your body contains DNA (deoxyribonucleic acid), the chemical compound that contains the genetic instructions on how to make you. DNA consists of two long chains of nucleotides twisted into a double helix which is held together by hydrogen bonds. The precise sequence of these nucleotides — the genes — determines the characteristics you inherit. A gene is one sequence of DNA that occupies a specific location on a chromosome and determines your individual characteristics — from the color of your eyes to your propensity for developing a particular illness.

Here's how DNA operates...

DNA self-replicates, copying genetic information to each new cell each time a cell divides, which is how we're able to make billions of new cells throughout our lives, yet remain fundamentally the same person. DNA also synthesizes or manufactures compounds from simple cell protein elements called RNA (ribonucleic acid), and transmits genetic information throughout our cells. In other words, DNA makes RNA, which makes proteins that the body uses to build individual characteristics, such as height, eye color, personality, and our risk of developing specific diseases and disorders.

Thanks to the Human Genome Project (HGP), we now have the complete map of all human genes. A genome is the full complement of an organism's genetic material (DNA sequencing) — the blueprint for building all the organism's structures and directing all the processes necessary to sustain the organism throughout life.

We humans have around 30,000 distinct genes residing on our 23 chromosome pairs. Prior to the completion of the HGP, we so vainly assumed that we were far more genetically sophisticated than all other creatures, but the joke's on us. Turns out, we share 98.7 percent of our genetic code with chimpanzees, for example. And while we are all different individuals, the genetic variation between any of us and Albert Einstein is actually less than 1 percent! But inside that narrow 1 percent differential you'll find an untold number of intellectual variations — not to mention physical and psychological variations.

While we are all of the same species, our genes have slight variations in structure, and these variations cause differences in our characteristics. Gene variations help explain why even members of the same family who may look alike and share other common characteristics are dramatically different in other significant ways, which could include, for instance, illnesses.

Some gene variations make us more vulnerable to certain disorders, others protect us from disorders. Some rare genetic diseases are

Science and the Effect of Genes on Depression

caused by variations in a single gene, but most common diseases are caused by a mixture of several gene variations and external factors, such as stress or toxic substances.

The difference between your physical appearance and your parents' illustrates the disparity in the actual amount of genetic material you share with each of them... and the difference between your genotype and your phenotype. Genotype is the entire set of genes you inherit — your biological potential. Phenotype refers to the observable properties of your body and your behavioral traits.

Your phenotype might be similar to your mother's, but your genotype is a 50–50 split from both parents. Your genotype may be predetermined, but your phenotype is a battle amongst your genes for control.

Some genes are dominant; that is, they only produce observable effects if they're present in either parent; a recessive gene will show up only if both parents possess it. The reason there are more brown-eyed people in the world than blue-eyed people is that the brown-eyed gene is dominant. If one parent contributes blue-eyed genes and the other brown-eyed genes, the child will have brown eyes unless — and here's where it gets complicated — a brown-eyed parent has a recessive gene for blue eyes lurking in the background that was passed along to the zygote. Since blue eyes are recessive, both parents must have contributed blue-eyed genes in order for their child to end up with blue eyes.

Green, grey and hazel eyes are also recessive, in case you're curious. Farsightedness dominates nearsightedness. Dark hair dominates blonde and red hair; a full head of hair dominates baldness. Freckles, dimples, double-jointedness and immunity to poison ivy are dominant.

You can see how gene dominance helps explain variations, and how it can have an impact on whether you inherit "undesirable" genes, or whether you dodge the bullet.

Is Emotional Resilience Genetic?

Why do stressful experiences lead to depression in some people but not in others? Several important genetic studies have found that a single gene called 5-HT T can moderate the influence of stressful life events on depression; in other words, your genetic makeup may help determine how much impact stress has on you.

The 5-HT T gene makes a protein that modifies a nerve cell's use of the chemical messenger serotonin, which is involved in regulating mood. (This is the protein that's inhibited by antidepressant medications.) 5-HT T has two variant forms, long and short. The short version of the gene has been linked to depression and anxiety. The long variant has been linked to emotional resilience.

The long and short of it is that 5-HT T predisposes some of us to depression, and protects others from it. People with either one or two short genes are likely to become depressed in response to multiple stressful experiences like death, divorce or assault, but they don't become depressed as long as they don't experience severe environmental stressors. In people with two long variants of 5-HT T, stress did not trigger depression, even if, for example, they've been severely mistreated in early childhood or suffered financial loss, poor health or deaths in the family.

In the predisposed, early trauma and subsequent adversity lead to depressive symptoms and subtle changes in the brain. Chronic depression produces marked changes in the brain. Certain structures begin to shrink or show structural disorganization. Resilience factors — perhaps including the protein produced by the 5-HT T gene, as well as conscious thought and behavioral modifications — can mitigate that damage or allow for repair.

Now, if you're hoping that you're one of the lucky ones who has two long genes, your odds are around 30 percent. Research thus far indicates that about 70 percent of us have at least one short 5-HT T gene, which may help explain why so many of us are vulnerable — or predisposed — to depression. But we also know that depression emerges from the interaction between genes and experience.

Other genes have been linked to depression, anxiety and resilience, and more genetic links will no doubt be discovered in the future. For example, researchers have identified gene variants that affect the expression of a signaling molecule called neuropeptide Y (NPY) that's known to be triggered by stress. NPY's release interacts with opioid compounds to help reduce anxiety and relieve pain. NPY also affects appetite, weight control and emotional responses.

People with the gene variant yielding the lowest NPY levels react with heightened emotion to stressful stimuli, which further illustrates why people vary in their resiliency to stress.

What Flips the Switch?

None of us is born a serial killer or a saint. We are not born depressed, anxious, manic or AD/HD. The influence of genes on behavior is indirect. The main job of genes is to build and organize the physical structures of the body, including the brain. These structures interact with the environment to produce behavior.

Throughout our lives, genes "express" themselves or turn on and off. Some genes are only expressed or "turned on" in response to stimuli from the outside world — environmental influences, lifestyle and geography. Like light switches, genes must receive electricity to turn on and express their particular proteins. So yes, genes create risk factors, but by themselves, they simply make proteins.

Scientists have identified specific genes and pathways that are affected by lifestyle and geography. These environmental factors can play a huge role in turning genes on or off. People who share the same genetic makeup but live in different environments may express genes differently. For example, our respiratory genes are "upregulated" or turned on more frequently in urban environments than in rural ones. The genes of urban dwellers, after all, must contend with greater pollution, which can contribute to respiratory diseases that the body naturally tries to ward off.

Studies that assess aspects of child-rearing such as physical punishment, hostility, lack of respect for the child's point of view, and unjustified criticism or humiliation provide another example of the gene-environment interaction. One Notre Dame study of male teens in a juvenile detention center investigated whether a gene associated with dopamine was more likely than a negative maternal parenting style to cause depression. The result? Neither factor alone predicted depression, but the boys who had especially rejecting mothers plus a certain form of the dopamine transporter gene were at higher risk for Major Depression and suicidal ideation.

Epigenetics: Altering Gene Expression
Meet the KRAB family...

The KRAB-ZFP family of genes is involved in regulating the expression of other genes and ultimately, for helping us deal with stress. The KRAB-ZFP genes, which appeared fairly recently on the evolutionary scale, serve as epigenetic censors, selectively silencing the expression of other genes. (Epigenetics refers to a change in gene expression that is caused by something other than a change in the underlying DNA sequence.)

These "repressors" make up about 2 percent of our genetic material, and vary from person to person. This variability in the KRAB family of regulators helps explain why some people are predisposed to anxiety or depression and some are not. Epigenetic alterations are often long-lasting or even permanent, so an individual's personal history can have a lasting impact on his or her genetic expression, like a sort of "cell memory."

In complex psychiatric disorders, many different genes may be involved in slightly increasing or decreasing risk of developing those disorders. Good genes may bequeath to us resources for coping with our environment, but a stressful environment can challenge even the most resilient genes. On the other hand, a stress-free environment can alter gene expression in a positive way. So can therapy.

Skills, behaviors and psychological disorders are shaped by both our biological inheritance and our life experiences. Your heredity gives you your potential, but it's your experience that determines how — and how much of — that potential is realized. In other words, psychological disorders are genetically influenced, but not genetically determined.

The Gene-Personality Connection

What about the interaction between genes, personality and temperament? Thanks to "imaging genomics" (e.g., MRI and fMRI), we can study the brain's workings in a way that helps us understand the genetic circuitry underlying diversity in human temperament and personality.

Beyond your genetic inheritance and environmental influences, there's another factor at work: the unique, individual, personal you. Anyone with children will tell you how different their biological children are from each other , even if they grew up in the same environment. One son loves sports and enjoys playing outdoors and the other prefers to stay indoors and would rather read and play video games. In fact, it's often said that parents with one child believe that upbringing determines personality, but parents with two children believe in genetic tendencies.

What connects our genetic inheritance to environmental experiences? One connection is personality, which is also subject, in part, to genes. Genes influence personality, and personality influences gene expression. Genetic predispositions interact with circumstances to produce unique individuals. Personality can be thought of as the sum of all the unique psychological qualities that influence a person's behavior across time and different situations.

People are drawn to particular environments because of their personalities. An extravert may prefer to spend her Saturday night at a party; an introvert may prefer to curl up with a good book.

We're learning that the same genes that predispose us to depression and anxiety can also make us more sensitive to negative environmental events and even increase our risk of experiencing negative events. Remember the 5-HT T gene? In addition to its link to depression and anxiety, the short variant of 5-HT T has also been linked to the personality trait neuroticism, which provoked some in the Media to dub 5-HT T "the Woody Allen gene." (Neuroticism is the tendency toward hand-wringing anxiety, instability, moodiness and negative thinking.)

Another example: nine different variations of the RGS2 gene have been associated with shy, inhibited behavior in children, introverted personality in adults, and increased activity in the amygdala and the insula, which process fear and anxiety. People with these RGS2 variants are at higher risk for anxiety disorders.

Many psychologists organize "personhood" or human personality traits into five dimensions, known as the "Big Five…" Extraversion, agreeableness, conscientiousness, emotional stability, and openness to experience. The idea is that when you describe someone's personality, what you're actually doing is unconsciously taking a measure of these five traits and crunching them together.

Emotional stability and conscientiousness appear to be directly related to physical and emotional well-being and longevity; in other words, wellness is linked to changes in these traits over time. Several studies have suggested that three traits — extraversion, neuroticism and openness to experience — can explain the heritability of life events. People who are extraverted and open to new experiences are more likely to experience positive and controllable life events, whereas people who are neurotic are more likely to experience negative life events — perhaps, in part, because they come to expect them. We often get what we expect in life.

We're all a little bit neurotic. Any mother will tell you that she has needlessly checked on her baby during naps to make sure the baby was still breathing! And who among us hasn't double-checked to make sure that a door was locked or that a stove burner was turned off? But we all have the capacity to turn neurotic, negative thinking into positive, hopeful thoughts. We actually have the capacity through our thoughts and behaviors to alter gene expression.

When we're trying to pinpoint whether variation within a particular population can be explained by genetic differences between individuals, we have to sort characteristics carefully. Nature and nurture can look a lot alike, and the personality variable always complicates matters.

People with similar personalities seek out similar experiences and may tend to take similar risks. For example, people who seek out excitement might be more inclined to participate in risky activities, which puts them at greater risk for getting into trouble, having traumatic accidents, getting sick, or other events that provoke depression and anxiety. Someone who's impulsive and prone to alcohol addiction is more likely to end up in bar fights than someone who has neither of these characteristics.

Much research has focused on how the "novelty-seeking" personality trait (impulsive, risk-taking, exploratory, thrill-seeking) relates to various psychological disorders. For example, those with high novelty-seeking characteristics are far more likely to become alcoholics, especially if they have an alcoholic parent. On the other hand, people with low novelty-seeking characteristics have a much lower risk of becoming alcoholics.

Someone with an aggressive, impulsive personality is also more likely to end up in bar fights. An "aggression" gene called MAOA is believed to influence how the brain gets wired during development. MAOA enzymes break down key mood-regulating chemical messengers, most notably serotonin. MAOA has two known variants that influence aggression and impulsiveness: the violence-related L version and its counterpart, the H version, which triggers less enzyme activity, thus leaving higher levels of serotonin in the brain.

By itself, the L variant of this gene is likely to contribute only a small amount of risk in interaction with other genetic and psychosocial influences; in other words, MAOA-L doesn't necessarily make people violent. But studying its effects in a large sample of "normal" people allows scientists to evaluate the heritability of aggressive personalities — how this gene variant biases the brain toward impulsive, aggressive behavior.

In reality, animals (which includes us!) actively seek out surroundings that are compatible with their genetic predispositions. Water moccasins look for excuses to slither into the water, though they can survive on land. Copperheads can swim, but they generally stick to dry habitats.

These predispositions don't necessarily have to be conscious or voluntary. A tall kid is more apt to be chosen for the basketball team and might end up being better at the game because he has more opportunity to develop his skills, not necessarily because he's a better player than a shorter kid.

Many studies have shown that the heritability of many psychological traits — from intelligence to depression and anxiety — increases as we mature. Now, this might seem counterintuitive at first blush, since we tend to think of genes as heavily influencing and molding us in early childhood. But here's the reason: As we get older, we become more able to determine our circumstances and more likely to choose environments that reinforce our natural personality tendencies — for better or for worse. And those environments influence our mental health, for better or for worse.

How Risky Is "Genetic Risk?"

Throughout the disorder assessment and treatment chapters in this book, you'll find statistics about genetic risk factors for depression. But bear in mind that statistics are always simple summaries about similarities amongst a group of people — they don't take into account all the individual characteristics of you.

The bottom line is that genes are never totally to blame for our fortunes, good or bad. Large-scale surveys of gene-environment-interaction research suggest that only around one-fourth of the variation between the mental health status of different individuals is heritable, which means that three-fourths is not. (Kendler, Baker, 2006) That means you have plenty of opportunity to influence your circumstances and decide whether or not you will, in fact, become your parents.

Can Your Personal Genome Predict Genes for "The Blues"?

How does genetic information help us? Identifying our individual susceptibility to certain conditions and pinpointing the specific factors that interact with this susceptibility to produce certain behaviors or diseases can empower us to take more control over our lives. Genetic histories do identify risk factors, but having a genetic risk for a disorder or disease does not mean that particular disorder or disease is inevitable. Behavior is always changeable, and is always affected by environment and experience.

Genetic information can also provide guidance for targeted screening efforts; for example, people who have a first-degree relative with a history of depression are at greater risk for developing depression themselves, especially when confronted with severe environmental stressors. But, as you'll learn in this book, taking proactive steps to combat depression before it sets in will help you defy the genetic odds.

You can have your personal genome mapped for around $2,200, a cost that's expected to drop to around $1000 within the next few years. But before you take the plunge, you might want to ask yourself this: Do I really want to know everything I could be at risk for? Even though we understand that genetic inheritance is not destiny, it's not unreasonable to assume that knowing you are at high risk for a debilitating illness can conceivably cheat you out of a quality life.

Gene scans can't tell you with certainty whether or not you will develop a particular mental health disorder. We don't yet know all the possible gene variations which may contribute to — or protect us from — mental health disorders. And we can't necessarily measure the degree to which other factors (e.g., environmental factors) contribute to disorder, or prevention of that disorder.

Your family history may provide the best clues about your genetic risk factors. Charting your own genogram is a great way to start.

Charting Your Own Mental Health History

Writing out your family history is a tool that can help you evaluate clinical, emotional and relational patterns over three or more generations.

As you work on your medical and mental health history, you will become conscious of how you've been influenced by your family of origin and will attempt to begin to make positive changes in your day-to-day life.

The health history questions will help you:

1. Identify your genetic risk factors for both physical and mental health disorders

2. Identify significant emotional and relationship patterns in your life that you need to work on

You can spend as much or as little time on your history as you wish. If you're interested in developing more comprehensive history than the ones provided in this book, you may want to investigate the genogram which graphically highlights family dynamics and use the software available at Genopro.com or Smartdraw.com.

Some therapists are trained to use genogram software, so if you find that you need more support while completing the genogram, a therapist can help you. It's a good idea for your therapist (if you have one) to take a look at your genograms.

Medical and Mental Health History

The Medical History and Mental Health History in the Appendix will allow you to take a closer look at your family history and assess your genetic risk for diseases and disorders. Remember, in order to get the right treatment, you must get the right diagnosis. Answering these questions may help you assess whether a medical condition is being misdiagnosed as a psychological problem, or vice versa. For example, hypothyroidism can be misdiagnosed as depression; hyperthyroidism can be misdiagnosed as mania. Alcohol and drug addiction (including prescription drug addiction) can mask mood disorders and exacerbate symptoms of any psychological disorder.

Once you've completed your Medical History and Mental Health History, look for patterns and note any concerns that you may have. Did you learn any new medical or psychiatric information that should be presented to your doctor or mental health professional? Are there any screening tests you should take? To ensure accuracy, you may want to verify details with each family member.

Emotional/Relational Health History

Are you emotionally "stuck"? The key to personal growth is moving from living life "unconsciously" to living with conscious awareness and understanding of your thoughts, feelings, and behaviors.

The Emotional/Relational Health History is a wonderful tool to include in your therapy process. It will shed light on troubled emotional and relationship patterns in your family history, which can help you quickly become aware of damaging patterns that need to be changed.

Build on your strengths. Look for the positive patterns and focus on being thankful for them. For example, let's say that you come from a family that often volunteers to do charitable work in the community. But your family life at home is less charitable and you need to find positive ways of connecting instead of criticizing each other. Identifying patterns in your family relationships can help you learn to treat each another with the empathy and charity with which you treat the people in the community.

11
How to Help Someone Who Needs Treatment

We all have a desire to reach out and help someone in need. But what does "help" mean? Extending help to someone with a mental health disorder can be complicated and challenging.

Often the person suffering doesn't know how to get their own needs met. Their psychological defense mechanisms can become so well-developed that they become experts at fooling people, and perhaps themselves. But defenses don't help them get better. They may be out of touch with their emotions and feelings, and may have lost the ability to connect to others, even — sometimes especially — those closest to them. Often, they won't or don't know how to communicate the depth of their agony and pain. They may fear that they will be rejected, and that admitting the problem will only trigger more negative consequences.

And so they keep going, untreated, hopeless, inadvertently spreading their pain to the people they care about most.

It's human nature to keep going. Most of us are not good at being sick — we don't know how to be sick. This is particularly true of people who are suffering from depression. Many people may not know they need treatment, don't know how to go about getting help, and might not have the energy or resources to take steps in the right direction.

People who are suffering from depression tend to be their own worst enemies, and often, it's necessary for someone to intervene. Luckily, more of us are getting involved in the psychological health of the people we care about. More than 90 percent of Americans say they'd be likely to contact or encourage a family member to consult with a mental health professional if needed. Your support can make all the difference.

Recovery is a partnership, and all parties must work toward the same goals: Restoring the mentally ill person, as well as your relationship, to good health. It's not your job to "fix" someone else.

Nor is it your job to make a diagnosis or determine an appropriate course of treatment. But you can offer positive, non-judgmental, practical support and connect the person to the necessary mental health resources. Think of that person as someone having a physical illness like diabetes or cancer. You probably wouldn't hesitate to call the doctor, make an appointment if they are unable to, and to help them comply with the necessary treatment.

First, encourage the person to assess where they are now by taking the Self-Questionnaire in the Appendix. If you have been in a position to observe the person's behavior frequently throughout the past few days, you may also want to take the Self-Questionnaire separately, answering the questions on the person's behalf.

Second, encourage the person to sit down and set goals, using the Treatment Goals worksheet in the Appendix.

The following strategies will help you broach the sensitive topic of seeking help, and map out a plan for moving forward toward an appropriate solution.

Practical Tips for Intervention

1. Cite clear examples of behavior that suggests disorder.
   For example:
   - I've noticed that you've been having a hard time getting out of bed every morning for the past month or so…
   - Lately, you seem to be more prone to making mistakes and forgetting things…

2. You may need to orchestrate a gentle intervention. Ask open-ended questions. Structure your conversation in such a way that you lead up to the topic gradually, gently. For example, if you suspect depression, it may not even be necessary to mention the word depression. You can frame your observations in the context of the person's demeanor, their apparent sluggishness, and the fact that they seem blue and "just not with it."
   For example:
   - Lately, you seem to be sad about a lot of things. How are you doing?…

- You don't seem to be very enthusiastic about your job [or relationship] anymore. Is there anything you want to talk about?...

3. Pay special attention to your communication style, including non-verbal behavior and gestures. Even though you may feel frustrated with the person, think about how they are hurting and treat them with loving words and kind gestures such as hugs and a welcoming posture. If the person views you as receptive and empathetic, they will be more likely to open up which can provide an opportunity for getting your loved one help.

4. Try to determine the cause of the person's behavior. Think about some of the possible reasons for the person's mood and/or behavior and use that with empathy to help the person recognize that they are under significant stress and it is legitimate to experience a range of emotions. That may help them move out of denial and begin to acknowledge their pain which is the first step to getting better.

5. Manage your own negative emotions so that you don't engage in self-defeating behavior. Try to control any impulse to react emotionally or defensively. For example, you may feel that the person has been unjustifiably angry and often criticizes you unfairly. Try not to view the criticism as a personal attack. Try to separate your personal ego from the situation.

   This could also be an opportunity for you to look at yourself and ask the question "Do I deserve any criticism?" Viewing yourself through the other person's eyes can bring to light your specific role and any unfavorable actions that may need to change. It may also help the person get better if you are able to recognize helpful ways that you might contribute to the problem.

6. Frame your issues/concerns in a helpful, positive context. Your goal is to create an atmosphere that lends itself to problem resolution. Try to view your relationship with the person as a

partnership, rather than viewing yourself as the victim of a power struggle. Be an ally, not an enemy.

Don't criticize. Discuss. There's a difference. Laying out your concerns in a non-adversarial way helps prevent further damage to the relationship. The odds of making the person angry and provoking a shut-down will be significantly reduced if you can discuss problems in a reasonable, diplomatic, non-defensive manner. If you've historically had a close personal relationship with the person, attempt to reestablish an emotional connection.

7. Still feel overwhelmed? Seek help from an objective therapist who can help you evaluate your options and bring in any other necessary professionals. Collaborating with a professional who has authority over the situation removes the responsibility of "fixing" someone from your shoulders and helps you manage your own stress.

What "support" is unhelpful?

Because discussing sensitive topics can feel awkward, it's easy to say and do the wrong thing. For example, it's not helpful to:
- Dismiss their mood or feelings, tell them "it's nothing," that they just need to "stay busy"
- Encourage them to "party" and numb painful feelings with alcohol or drugs
- Criticize, belittle, threaten or be judgmental

The Breakdown: Managing a Crisis

If someone close to you is suicidal, your support can literally be a matter of life and death. Understanding the risk factors and warning signs can help you make an informed evaluation of the person's behavior.

Risk factors for suicide include:
- Major Depression, Bipolar Disorder and/or Substance-Abuse Disorder or other serious mental disorders such as psychotic disorders. More than 90 percent of people who die by suicide

- suffer from depression and/or have substance abuse problems.
- Stressful life events, in combination with other risk factors, such as depression. Stressors might include divorce, separation, bereavement, chronic illness or medical condition, loss of job)
- Previous suicide attempt or gesture
- Family history of mental health disorder or substance abuse
- Family history of suicide
- Family violence, including physical or sexual abuse
- Firearms in the home (guns are used in 50 percent of all suicides)
- Incarceration
- Exposure to the suicidal behavior of others, such as family members, peers, or celebrity figures
- No social support system (e.g., family, friends)
- Low levels of serotonin in the brain. Decreased serotonin levels have been found in the brains of suicide victims, as well as people with depression and impulse control disorders.

Suicide and suicidal behavior are not normal responses to severe stress. Many people live with these risk factors, but are not suicidal. Risk factors do not guarantee that someone will commit suicide. They only increase the chances that someone might.

If You Believe Someone is Suicidal...

Case Vignette

A 35-year-old woman began to sink into despair following a devastating divorce. Loneliness and sadness drove her to have an affair with a married man which resulted in pregnancy, an abortion, and another breakup. For several months, she had thoughts of suicide.

As a nurse, she was able to obtain medications that she knew would result in death. One night, a neighbor overhead her arguing with her sister on the phone. She hung up the phone, swallowed enough pills and died. She had few friends and told no one about her plan. There were no cries for help, no one to intervene.

Sometimes there's a straw that breaks the camel's back...

It can happen right in front of you... someone you care about in crisis, crying uncontrollably, or perhaps staring off into the distance, disconnected, unable to think for themselves or perform even the simplest tasks.

How do you help someone in crisis?

The best strategy for crisis management, of course, is prevention. People who have had the benefit of therapeutic oversight are likely to be more resilient, better able to cope with new stressors, and less vulnerable to "breaking down" in the first place.

But what do you do if someone is in crisis and there's no therapist to call?

The first thing to know about suicidal intervention is this: There's no such thing as "overreacting." Anyone who talks about committing suicide should be taken seriously. Anyone who is thinking about committing suicide needs immediate attention from a mental health professional.

The fact that someone is in crisis does not necessarily mean they are on the brink of suicide. These warning signs will help you evaluate the risk:

- Talking about feeling suicidal or wanting to die
- Feeling hopeless, that nothing will ever change or get better
- Feeling helpless, that nothing anyone does makes a difference
- Feeling like a burden to family and friends
- Feeling extreme, chronic fatigue, coupled with depression
- Abusing alcohol or drugs
- Putting affairs in order (e.g., organizing finances, giving away possessions, visiting friends or family members one last time)
- Organizing a plan for suicide (e.g., method, date)
- Buying instruments of suicide (e.g., gun, rope, medications)
- Writing a suicide note
- Intentionally putting oneself in harm's way, or in situations

where there is a danger of being killed (e.g., "suicide by cop")

In evaluating suicide risk, therapists always look for suicide ideation. Suicidal ideation is defined as thoughts of taking one's own life with some degree of intent. If someone has had suicidal ideation, it does not necessarily mean that the person is an imminent risk to self. Someone who has a plan for how they will commit suicide needs to be carefully monitored.

What's the difference between a suicide attempt and a suicidal gesture?

A suicidal gesture is a suicide attempt in which the person has no intent to die; for example, the person may take a non-lethal dose of sleeping pills or cut themselves in ways not likely to cause imminent death (the latter is often referred to as "small cuttings"). The intent of a suicide gesture is generally to express despair or helplessness or to utter a desperate cry for help in an effort to improve one's life, not to die. In some cases, a suicide gesture may be an attempt to make a dramatic statement or "get even with someone;" this most commonly occurs among people with personality disorders, such as Borderline Personality Disorder.

A suicidal attempt may be a failed suicide; for example, the person may ingest a bottle of pills with the intent to die, but someone intervened, called an ambulance and the person wakes up alive in the hospital, having had their stomach pumped. Others may intend to die but choose a method that's inadequate to bring death. For example, a person may drive a car off a steep cliff, certain that they'll be killed, but somehow manage to survive the wreck.

Suicide attempts and gestures can look a lot alike. Either way, the person needs professional help. Gestures may eventually become attempts, and attempts will eventually be successful.

While some suicide attempts are carefully planned over time, others are impulsive acts that have not been well thought out. Many people who complete suicide don't tell anyone in the preceding months, including their therapist. However, if the suicidal person has been under the close care of a therapist, there's a good chance that the therapist will figure it out — even if the person won't admit it —

and can then determine the appropriate way to handle the situation.

Case Vignette

John was a successful architect who loved his career and took pride in his role as provider for his wife and three children. Then came the car accident, and debilitating injuries... his right hand was permanently damaged; he could no longer draft architectural plans, or even write — he could no longer be an architect. He lost his job and gradually sank into a deep depression. No longer the able provider, he began to believe that he was worthless to his family, and had recurring thoughts of harming himself.

But his wife persuaded him to see a therapist, and a psychiatrist prescribed an antidepressant. Both professionals required him to agree to a contract: he must promise to call if his thoughts of suicide turned into plans. One bleak night, John did, in fact, begin to plan an exit; he would drive his car over the edge of a cliff. He called his therapist and was admitted into psychiatric care. He was motivated to get help because he knew how much it would hurt his wife and children if he harmed himself. After a few months of treatment and family support, his mood improved, his outlook on life became more optimistic. He began to investigate other ways to earn a living. He learned to view his challenge as an opportunity for change and growth.

What to do if you're not sure whether someone is suicidal

When in doubt, reach out. In other words, always stay on the side of caution. These tips can help you help the person, while evaluating suicidal risk...

- Encourage the person to talk to you and tell you how he/she feels. Be willing to listen for as long as the person needs to talk. Make them feel comfortable about expressing their feelings. Accept and validate their feelings. Don't be judgmental or instruct the person on how to behave. Don't debate whether suicide is "right" or "wrong," or whether their feelings are "good" or "bad." Don't lecture on the "value of life."

- Look for suicide ideation. Be direct. Talk openly about suicide. Ask: "Are you thinking about hurting yourself? Are you thinking about suicide?" If the answer is yes, ask: "Have you considered it recently? Do you have a plan?"
- Never dare him/her to do it, even in the heat of an argument.
- Don't act shocked; this can cause the person to feel rejected and pull away from you.
- Don't offer glib reassurances; this only makes the person feel that you don't understand.
- Encourage the person to schedule stress-relieving activities every day, such as exercise, prayer, meditation or journaling. Socializing with others can help prevent isolation.
- Never agree to be "sworn to secrecy." Seek help.

If you are feeling suicidal or know someone who is:
- Reach out for immediate help. Call a doctor, 911 right away. Reach out to agencies specializing in crisis intervention and suicide prevention, such as National Suicide Prevention Lifeline: 1-800-273-TALK (8255). Someone is available to help 24/7. This service is available to everyone, and you may call for yourself or for someone you care about. All calls are confidential.
- Make sure you (or the suicidal person) are not left alone
- Remove potentially lethal medication, guns, knives and other weapons or items from the home.

What happens after a suicide attempt?

In many cases, the suicidal person may need to be hospitalized until the danger of additional attempts has passed. A therapist can evaluate the risks and determine the safest course of action.

Following a psychiatric hospitalization, suicide prevention measures usually include a comprehensive outpatient treatment plan, hopefully leading to a final discharge. It's critical that the suicidal person comply with the outpatient treatment plan in order to prevent additional suicide attempts and keep the person on the road to recovery. Intensive treatment of the underlying psychological disorder will decrease both short-term and long-term risk. Therapy which focuses on helping the person understand how their thoughts impact behaviors, can be an effective treatment for people who struggle with thoughts of harming themselves.

For suicidal teens and adolescents, school intervention programs may help provide support and education about risk factors, symptoms, and ways to manage suicidal thoughts. Such programs also help teach kids how to engage adults when they or a friend expresses suicidal thinking.

The most important thing to keep in mind is that suicidal feelings and actions are symptoms of an illness that can be treated. With proper treatment, suicidal feelings can be overcome.

12
Conclusion:
The Truth Shall Make You Free

Truth is not always pretty, delicate or welcomed. It is not often delivered in a whole or impeccable condition. Sometimes, it takes a little time, patience and deeper analysis to arrive at the heart of the matter. And that's what the diagnostic and therapeutic processes are all about: seeking, finding, accepting, healing.

Sometimes it's easier to live in denial, for as long as you can get by with it. Many people stay in denial because they adapt to their depression and forget what it feels like to be happy. Sadly, denial keeps people trapped in the struggle to find peace, purpose, and contentment and ultimately leads to more pain and a more difficult to treat illness. Breaking through denial is one of the hardest parts of conquering depression. The first step to effectively treat an illness is to acknowledge that you have one.

I admire you for taking the step to read and explore information that could help you find the right treatment. Your courage and willingness to seek solutions demonstrates your capacity for making choices that will ultimately facilitate healing. If you've read this entire book, it's likely that you now understand what you're dealing with. Maybe you feel overwhelmed and need some time to sort through it all. Hopefully, this book has provided you confidence in making decisions — from choosing the right therapist to evaluating your treatment options.

You are no longer stuck. You are already moving towards healing and health.

Here are some final thoughts to keep in mind as you continue your journey of self-discovery, wherever that journey may lead you…

Knowledge is power. Information is empowering, whether it feels like it or not as you're receiving it, even if what you have learned is not what you wanted to hear. The instant that you fully understand what you're dealing with, it has just relinquished some of its power over you. And then you have the ability to make decisions that could

Conclusion: The Truth Shall Make You Free

help you feel better.

A person is more than their diagnosis. Once someone is diagnosed with depression, it's easy to lose sight of all the other unique aspects of that person. In my work with clients, I have never seen any one person with depression look exactly the same as another. We are all different. No one fits perfectly into any diagnostic category.

A diagnosis, in the end, is nothing more than the first step towards choosing the most helpful treatment for a disorder — a cluster of symptoms, patterns of thought and behavior. A person is so much more than that. The person is not the illness, and the illness is not the person.

The sooner, the better...this is the case for every disease and disorder in the world. Imagine how many cancer patients regret not getting help earlier, before the cancer became terminal? Facing and acknowledging your problems early almost certainly guarantees that treatment will be more effective and take less time to be successful, no matter whether the treatment is therapy, medications, natural treatments, or all three. The more severe the symptoms, the more difficult they are to treat.

Remember that even the most severe symptoms began as mild. Mild symptoms, left untreated, can progress to severe.

Competence counts.

Without the right diagnosis, it will be difficult to get the right treatment. Choose the mental health provider who's right for you. Choose someone who is empathetic, objective and has the right credentials and experience for your symptoms. Finding the right people to support you in your treatment is a major key to success.

Genetically influenced, not genetically determined.

Your genetic inheritance may create biological potential, but it's your experience that determines how that potential is expressed. Even if your mental health history suggests that your gene pool may be influencing your symptoms, remember: You have the power to alter gene expression. The right treatment(s) can move you in a new direction.

Whatever your preconceived notions were about therapy, natural treatments, or medications, I encourage you to learn as much as you can about yourself with an open mind and find the best treatment for you.

It is my hope that reading this book has been a transformative process for you, and that your newfound knowledge will help you transcend the limitations that are preventing you from achieving your highest potential — spiritually, personally, relationally, and professionally. If this book has confirmed your suspicions, at least you will know the truth, and the truth, applied thoughtfully and skillfully, will make you free.

Appendix:

Depression Quiz: Self-Questionnaire

This questionnaire will help you assess whether you may be depressed. Choose the answer that best reflects your mood over a two week period.

1. I've been crying more than usual.
   A Yes
   B Sometimes
   C No

2. I get very little sleep or I sleep too much.
   A Yes
   B Sometimes
   C No

3. I feel that I am worthless — a failure.
   A Yes
   B Sometimes
   C No

4. I don't like myself.
   A Yes
   B Sometimes
   C No

5. I feel very guilty and responsible for things that are happening to myself and others.
   A Yes
   B Sometimes
   C No

6. I have trouble concentrating or thinking clearly.
   A Yes
   B Sometimes
   C No

7. My appetite has increased or decreased.
   A Yes
   B Sometimes
   C No

8. I'm not enjoying activities that I normally enjoy.
   A Yes
   B Sometimes
   C No

9. My energy is low, I feel fatigued. It find it difficult to get out of bed in the morning.
   A Yes
   B Sometimes
   C No

10. I feel sad most of the time.
    A Yes
    B Sometimes
    C No

11. I have the sense that something bad is going to happen.
    A Yes
    B Sometimes
    C No

12. I find it hard to do simple things, and often have to force myself to do them.
    A Yes
    B Sometimes
    C No

13. I've been thinking about harming myself.
    A Yes
    B Sometimes
    C No

Apendix

Scoring Instructions:

A = 2 points, B = 1 point, C = 0 point. Total your points from the 12 questions.

NOTE: If you answered Yes to Question #13, please seek help immediately from a mental health provider. Suicidal ideation is an indicator of severe depression.

18-26 points You have some significant indicators of depression. See a mental health provider for further assessment.

12-18 points You have some symptoms of mild depression. To ensure that your symptoms are not getting worse, re-take this test weekly, and continue to use the Depression Mood Chart to chart your daily moods. You may want to pursue therapy to learn how to better cope with problems and stress.

Under 12 points You appear to have a healthy outlook on life and your mood is within the normal range.

Note: If you have had these symptoms in a milder form for 2 years or more, you may have dysthymia, a milder form of depression.

IMPORTANT NOTE: This self-questionnaire is not intended to be used as a diagnostic tool. Rather, it's meant to provide a framework that will help you become aware of your symptoms and begin to develop an action plan.

If you believe that you may be depressed, your next step is to seek out a competent mental health professional who can provide an accurate diagnosis and help you develop a treatment plan that works for you.

Medical and Mental Health History

Having a medical and mental health history from family members will provide you insight into your own physical concerns and will make it easier for your doctor or therapist to diagnose what you are dealing with.

First, answer each of the following questions about yourself, then ask each member of your family to provide answers about themselves.

1. What illnesses, hospitalizations, or diseases have you experienced in your lifetime?

2. Is there anything genetically that you might be more prone to because of your family history?

3. Have you ever had any psychological disorders — however brief — including depression, anxiety, bipolar disorder, or AD/HD?

4. Have you ever had any thoughts of suicide or attempted suicide? (This question helps screen depression risk)

5. Are you addicted to alcohol, drugs (prescription drugs), or any other harmful substance?

Emotional/Relational History

Taking the time to understand your family history emotionally and relationally will be very helpful to you as you uncover patterns of thinking or relating that you would like to change. Often the roots will be found in your childhood, and once you are conscious of these patterns, you will be able to change them more easily.

First, answer each of the following questions about yourself, then ask each member of your family to provide answers about themselves.

1. Describe yourself in 3 words. One word should reflect how you deal with your feelings (e.g., do you hold them in, discuss them openly in healthy ways, or yell or scream and express them in unhealthy ways)?

2. Evaluate closeness and distance between different family members. For example, are your parents close, distant or conflictual? Were there any incidents of physical, emotional, or sexual abuse? What are the positive values and behaviors among your family members?

Name _____ Month _____ Year _____

Mood Chart for DEPRESSION

DAYS	1	2	3	4	5	6	7	8	9	10	11	12	13	14	15	16	17	18	19	20	21	22	23	24	25	26	27	28	29	30	31
Severe — Significant impairment, Notable to work																															
Moderate — Significant impairment, Able to work																															
Mild — Without significant impairment																															
Normal																															
Anxiety (0 - None, 1 - Mild, 2 - Moderate, 3 - Severe)																															
Hours Slept																															
Natural Remedies																															
Medication (name / mg)																															

Mood Trigger at the back

Days	Mood Triggers
1	
2	
3	
4	
5	
6	
7	
8	
9	
10	
11	
12	
13	
14	
15	
16	
17	
18	
19	
20	
21	
22	
23	
24	
25	
26	
27	
28	
29	
30	
31	

Treatment Goal Planning Worksheets

You've probably heard the old expression "Start with the end in mind." Setting treatment goals allows you to quickly map out a path to progress and develop a framework for therapy.

Goals motivate us to do better, get better and adhere to the treatment plan. Goals provide structure and focus. They prevent us from getting stuck and help both therapist and client stay focused on the primary issues.

The client and therapist together will determine what the primary struggles are with regards to family of origin issues, current stressors, emotional symptoms, relationship conflicts, self-worth, basically anything that is causing distress. No individual will have exactly the same issues or goals that you have. You will want to make sure and tailor your treatment plan specifically for you and ask your therapist to create interventions that address your needs. This process can be as simple or complicated as you like.

Your treatment goals should be reviewed regularly — every 6 to 8 weeks is a good rule of thumb. Why? First, to monitor your progress. Second, you may find that your needs and priorities evolve over time and your goals may need to be adjusted to accommodate them.

Sample Treatment Goals for Depression
Concern: Sad, crying a lot. Isolated. Trouble sleeping.
Goal: I want to sleep well, have a positive mood and lots of good friends.

Concern: Negative thoughts. I feel like a failure.
Goal: I want to learn to manage my negative thoughts and replace them with more positive thoughts and feelings. I want to be and feel successful.

Concern: Fighting with my mother causes me great distress.
Goal: I want to understand the patterns in my family of origin, so I can change how I relate to my mother. I want a healthy relationship with my mother.

Treatment Goal Planning Worksheets

In setting your goals, ask yourself two questions:
1. What are the specific concerns that brought me to therapy?
2. For each concern, what is the positive outcome I want to accomplish?

Concern: _____

Goal: _____

Concern: _____

Goal: _____

Concern: _____

Goal: _____

Concern: _____

Goal: _____

Concern: _____

Goal: _____

Concern: _____

Goal: _____

Concern: _____

Goal: _____

Bibliography

Beck, Aaron T. & Alford, Brad A. Depression: Causes and Treatment. Pennsylvania: University of Pennsylvania Press, 2009.

Burns, David. Feeling Good. New York: HarperCollins Publisher, 1980.

Copeland, Mary Ellen. The Depression Workbook. Oakland, CA: New Harbinger Publications, 2001.

Diagnostic and Statistical Manual of Mental Disorders, Fourth Edition Text Revision (DSM-IV-TR). American Psychiatric Association. 2000.

Kendler, K.S., Baker, J.H.. Virginia Institute for Psychiatric and Behavioral Genetics, Department of Psychiatry, Medical College of Virginia of Virginia Commonwealth University, Richmond, VA 23298-0126, USA, 2006.

Knaus, William. The Cognitive Behavioral Workbook for Depression. Oakland, CA: New Harbinger Publications, Inc, 2006.

(NIMH) U.S. Department of Health and Human Services. Mental Health: A Report of the Surgeon General. Rockville, MD: U.S. Department of Health and Human Services, Substance Abuse and Mental Health Services Administration, Center for Mental Health Services, National Institutes of Health, National Institute of Mental Health, 1999.

National Institutes of Health, New Therapies Show Promise for Vascular Depression, May 7, 2008. http://nimh.nih.gov/science-news/2008/

O'Connor, Richard. Undoing Depression. Berkley, CA: Little, Brown and Company, Inc., 1999.

Solomon, Andrew. Noonday Demon. New York: Scribner, 2001.

LaVergne, TN USA
21 November 2010

205786LV00001B/53/P